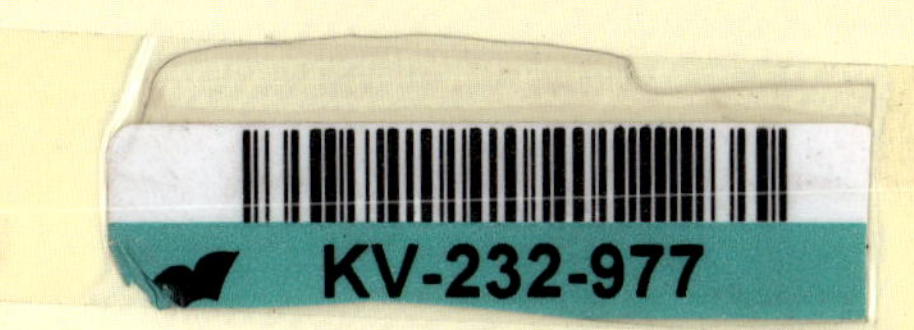

LOOKING AT Language

Brian Keaney and Bill Lucas

Published by the Press Syndicate of the University of Cambridge
The Pitt Building, Trumpington Street, Cambridge CB2 1RP
40 West 20th Street, New York, NY 10011–4211, USA
10 Stamford Road, Oakleigh, Melbourne 3166, Australia

First published 1994

Printed in Great Britain at the University Press, Cambridge

A catalogue record for this book is available from the British Library
ISBN 0 521 43764 4 paperback

Picture research by Callie Kendall
Illustrations by: Linda Combi (pages 5, 29, 45, 84, 85); Maggie Ling (pages 34, 66, 74–5, 76); Sharon Scotland (pages 20, 23, 36–7, 87); Sue Shields (pages 8, 12, 13, 14, 15, 17, 81).

Acknowledgements
Thanks are due to the following for permission to reproduce photographs:

Cover: *top*, courtesy of Lytton Enterprises Limited, Knebworth House; *bottom*: photo by Tick Ahearn/courtesy of Claire Harrison and BBC Radio Cambridgeshire

8, 92*tl*, 92*b*, by permission of the British Library, London; 10, Tapisserie de Bayeux et avec autorisation spéciale de la Ville de Bayeux; 11, E.T. Archive/by permission of the Board of Trustees of the Victoria & Albert Museum; 7, 13, 24*b*, 25, 27*b*, 33, 34, 35*r*, 40(*fax*), 40*tc*, 40*tr*, 96, 97, 120, Michael Brooke; 16, courtesy of Lytton Enterprises Limited, Knebworth House; 19, photo by Michael Brooke/courtesy of Cambridge Museum of Technology; 22, 26*t*, E.T. Archive; 24*t*, from The Great Bible, by permission of the Syndics of the Cambridge University Library; 26*bl*, 27*t*, from *Hewes: A Perfect Survey of the English Tongue*, 1624, by permission of the Syndics of the Cambridge University Library; 26*br*, from *Bullokar: Booke at Large & Bref Grammar*, 1586, by permission of the Syndics of the Cambridge University Library; 32, by courtesy of the National Portrait Gallery, London; 35*l*, from *Noah Webster: An American Dictionary of the English Language*, 1828, by permission of the Syndics of the Cambridge University Library; 40*tl*, Mary Evans Picture Library; 40(*newspaper*), ©Viewfinder Colour Photo Library; 40*b*, M & V Birley/Tropix; 41*t*, 42, Popperfoto; 41*b*, Imperial War Museum, London; 41*c*, Topham Picture Source; 43*r*, Novosti Photo Library (London); 43*l*, 48*tc*, 48*tr*, 48*bc*, 48*br*, 49, 52, 59, 73, 119(*judge*), 119*br*, Rex Features; 44, P. Frances/Tropix; 48*tl*, 48*bl*, © Monitor Syndication; 50, 119(*weatherman*), ©BBC Photo Library; 58*l*, ©The Financial Times Ltd/Robert Harding Picture Library; 58*r*, Robert Harding Picture Library; 63, reproduced from the Ladybird title *Let Me Write* by W. Murray, illustrated by Martin Aitchison, with the permission of the publishers, Ladybird Books Limited/photo by Michael Brooke; 77, *Le Regard intérieur* by Rene Magritte, ©ADAGP, Paris and DACS, London 1994/Bridgeman Art Library; 92*tr*, from *Quentin Blake's ABC*, Cape, 1989, by permission of the Syndics of the Cambridge University Library; 97*bl*, from *Shakespeare: A Facsimile of the First Folio Text*, 1623, by permission of the Syndics of the Cambridge University Library; 97*br*, from *Bacon: Proficience and Advancement of Learning*, by permission of the Syndics of the Cambridge University Library; 118*t*, Aerofilms, Ltd.; 118*b*, Alan Weaving/Ardea, London; 119(*scientist*), Robert Irving; 119*tr*, Wolfshead/Ben Osborne/Ardea, London; 119*tl*, Jim Holmes/Panos Pictures; 119*bl*, P. Morris/Ardea, London; 124, 125, ©ASAP/Israel Talby

Contents

diabetes (*say* dy-a-**bee**-teez) *noun* a dis-

wicked. **2** very clever or annoying.

diadem (*say* **dy**-a-dem) *noun* a crown or headband worn by a royal person.

diagnose *verb* (**diagnosed, diagnosing**) find out what disease a person has or what is wrong. **diagnosis**, *noun*, **diagnostic** *adjective*.

diagonal (*say* dy-**ag**-on-al) *noun* a straight line joining opposite corners **diagonal** *adjective*, **diagonally** *adverb* [fr
+ Greek *gonia* = angle]

Starting point

diagram *noun* a king of drawing or picture that shows the parts of something or how it works. [from *dia-* + *-gram*]

dial *noun* a circular object with numbers or letters round it.

dial *verb* (**dialled, dialling**) telephone a number by turning a telephone dial or pressing numbered buttons.

dialect *noun* the words and pronunciation used by people in one district but not in the rest of a country.

dialogue *noun* a conversation.

dialysis (*say* dy-**al**-iss-iss) *noun* a way of removing harmful substances from the blood by letting it flow through a machine. [from *dia-*, + Greek *lysis* = loosening]

diameter (*say* dy-**am**-it-er) *noun* **1** a line drawn straight across a circle or sphere and passing through its centre. **2** the length of this line. [from Greek, = measuring across]

diametrically *adverb* completely, *diametrically opposite*.

diamond *noun* **1** a very hard precious stone that looks like clear glass. **2** a shape with four equal sides and four angles that are not right angles. **3** a playing-card with red diamond shapes on it. [from Greek *adamas* = adamant (= a very hard stone)].

diaper *noun* a baby's nappy.

diaphanous (say dy-**af**-an-us) *adjective* (or fabric) almost transparent.

diaphragm (*say* **dy**-a-fram) *noun* **1** the muscular partition inside the body that separates the chest from the abdomen and is used in breathing.

bowels. [from *dia-*, + Greek rhoia = a

book in
what hap-
s = day]

diatribe *noun* a strong verbal attack.

dice *noun* strictly this is the plural of **die²**, but is often used as a singular, *plural* **dice** a small cube marked with dots (1 to 6) on its sides, used in games.

dice *verb* (**diced, dicing**) **1** play gambling games using dice. **2** cut into small cubes.

dictate *verb* (**dictated, dictating**) **1** say or read something aloud for some one to write down. **2** give orders in an officious way. **dictation** noun [from Latin dictare = keep saying]

dictates (*say* **dik**-tayts) plural noun order, commands.

dictator *noun* a ruler who has unlimited power, **dictatorial** (*say* dik-ta-**tor**-ee-al) *adjective*, **dictatorship** *noun*.

diction *noun* a person's way of speaking words, *clear diction*.

dictionary *noun* (*plural* **dictionaries**) a book that contains words in alphabetical order so that you can find out how to spell them and what they mean. [from Latin *dictio* = word]

didactic (*say* dy-**dak**-tik) *adjective* having the manner of someone who is lecturing people, **didactically** *adverb* [from Greek *didaktikos* = teaching]

diddle *verb* (**diddled, diddling**) (*slang*) cheat; swindle.

didn't (*mainly spoken*) did not.

die¹ *verb* (**died, dying**) **1** stop living or existing. **2** stop burning or functioning, *The fire had died down*.

die² *noun* singular of dice.

die³ *noun* a device that stamps a design on coins etc. or that cuts or moulds metal.

die-hard *noun* a person who obstinately refuses to give up old ideas or policies.

diesel (*say* **dee**-zel) *noun* **1** an engine that works by burning oil in compressed air. **2** fuel for this kind of engine. [named after a German engineer, R. Diesel]

diet¹ *noun* **1** special meals that someone eats in order to be healthy or to become less fat. **2** the sort of foods usually eaten by a person or animal.

A **dictionary** is an essential piece of equipment for anyone wishing to get to grips with language. There are many different kinds of dictionary. The one here has been published for young people of your age.

It tells you:

- what a word means
- when the plural of a word is not made by simply adding the letter 's'
- how to say difficult words
- where some words came from
- what kind of word you are dealing with
- whether a word is mainly used in spoken English
- how words are spelled
- where the same word has a number of different meanings.

Although no two dictionaries look exactly the same, once you have understood the main purposes of a dictionary, you will easily be able to use different kinds.

Investigate

Find out how many different English dictionaries there are:

a in your home

b in your English classroom

c in your school's library

d in your local library.

Anglo-Saxon beginnings AD 500–1100

English has not always been the same as it is today. Over the last two and a half thousand years, many different languages have been spoken in the British Isles. From this jigsaw puzzle of languages, Modern English has emerged.

More than two thousand years ago, the people who lived here were called Celts. They spoke languages similar to Modern Welsh or Gaelic.

Between 55 BC and AD 410 the Romans lived in parts of the British Isles. They spoke a language called Latin. But, although some Celts learned Latin so that they could work for the Romans, the Celtic languages remained largely unaffected. Even now, Celtic survives in Wales, Scotland and Ireland. It died out as a natural native language in Cornwall two hundred years ago and a few years ago in the Isle of Man.

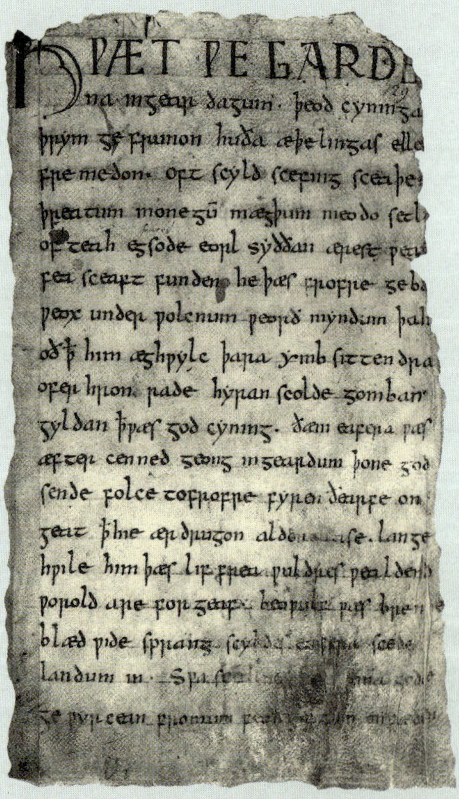

In AD 449 a number of tribes invaded what we now call England. They came from the north of Germany and were called Saxons, Jutes and Angles. The languages they spoke were similar to each other and gradually became called 'Englisc' (the language of the Angles, or Old English, as it has since been called). This language rapidly became the main one used in Britain, and the Celtic-speaking peoples were restricted to the West and North. It is commonly known as **Anglo-Saxon**, a name made by combining the names of two of these tribes.

Anglo-Saxon or Old English looks different from Modern English for three main reasons:

1 Some of the letters were different:

- the sound for which we now use the letter 'w' was indicated by the letter 'wynn' which looked quite like the modern 'p'
- the letters 'þ' and 'ð' were used for the two different 'th' sounds which are found at the beginning of the words 'thin' and 'this'
- 'a' was often pronounced rather differently, almost like the 'e' in 'get'. To get the 'a' sound in 'cat', they used 'ae'.

2 Many verbs began with the letters 'ge-'. Starting a word with 'ge-' was a way of showing that the action being described had been completed. For example, *climban* meant 'to climb', but *geclimban* showed that the climber had reached the top.

3 The same words could be given different endings. The word for good, *gode*, could appear as *godne*, *godes* or *godra*. This was because Old English was an **inflected language**. An inflected language is one in which parts of words change to show a different meaning. If you learn German you will become familiar with this idea. To a lesser extent, this type of change occurs in French and Spanish as well. Most types of inflection have died out in Modern English, although some types of word do still change. For example, we say 'I will climb the hill tomorrow', but 'I climbed the hill yesterday'. The '-ed' ending shows that the verb 'climb' is being used in the past tense. Can you think of any other examples of words changing their endings because the speaker wants to change their meaning in a sentence?

Activity

How much of the extract on the opposite page do you recognise? It may help you to read it aloud in pairs, helping each other to guess at words which seem difficult. (You might be interested to know that most Anglo-Saxons could not have done as well as you – very few of them could read or write!)

The Norman invasion

A panel from the Bayeux tapestry, which was embroidered c.1067–77.

Everyone has heard of 1066 and William the Conqueror. Perhaps few of us realise the long-term effects this invasion had on the English language.

'For a man know French, men count him of little. But low men hold to English and to their own speech yet.'

Robert of Gloucester

You have already seen how, when the Anglo-Saxons arrived, their language rapidly replaced Celtic. It would, therefore, be reasonable to assume that the same thing would have happened again, and that Norman French would have replaced Old English.

In fact this did not happen, for three main reasons:

1. Old English or Anglo-Saxon was too well established.
2. The French soldiers began to marry English women and in this way learned the local language.
3. Fighting for control of southern England and northern France kept the nobles very busy and meant that they were unable to spend much time establishing their own customs in England.

This time the changes to the language were more subtle. Those who wanted to be successful adopted French as their language. But many ordinary people continued to use English.

Middle English AD 1100–1500

As a result of this, a new language began to be formed. Slowly, Old English and Old French merged together into a language which we now call **Middle English** – a step closer to the language we use today.

In 1362, for the first time, English was used to open Parliament. After nearly three hundred years, this was an indication that what we now call Middle English had finally become established.

At about the same time, Geoffrey Chaucer began to write *The Canterbury Tales* and other books. French was still the main language of government, but Chaucer chose to write in English. Many people read Chaucer's books, and his influence on the English language was considerable.

A Knight ther was, and that a worthy man,
That fro the tyme that he first bigan
To ryden out, he loved chivalrye,
Trouthe and honour, fredom and curteisye.
Ful worthy was he in his lordes werre,
And thereto hadde he riden (no man ferre)
As wel in Cristendom as hethenesse,
And ever honoured for his worthinesse.
At Alisaundre he was, whan it was wonne;
Ful ofte tyme he hadde the bord bigonne
Aboven alle naciouns in Pruce ...
And evermore he hadde a sovereyn prys.
And though that he were worthy, he was wys,
And if his port as meke as is a mayde
He never yet no vileinye ne sayde
In al his lyf, unto no maner wight.
He was a verray parfit gentil knight.

Activity

Read this aloud. How much of it can you understand?
Make a list of the ways in which it is different from:

a the Old English extract on page 8
b Modern English.

Who stole that word?

In the *Oxford English Dictionary* there are more than five hundred thousand words. Words are the vital ingredient of language, able to surprise, shock or persuade us. But where do they all come from?

Read this extract about an unlikely private eye.

So long, Harry

Harry Fink, the world's most unfashionable detective, walked into the Happy Zebra bar. 'I'd like a vodka and sherbet,' he told the bartender.

The bartender shrugged and did as he was told. He looked the stranger up and down as he wiped the glass clean. He was of medium height and medium build with a very forgettable face. But no one could forget his clothes sense. He wore red dungarees under a bright green anorak. Over his shoulder he carried a ukulele.

'You planning to give us a song?' the bartender asked.

'I'm looking for the yodelling killer,' Harry replied, 'I'm told you might know something about him.'

The bartender leaned closer to Harry. 'You mean the thug who's been going around bumping off opera singers?'

Harry nodded.

'He's across the street in the Bamboo Grove restaurant eating a hamburger with plenty of tomato sauce.'

Harry drained his glass. 'Can I make a call from here?' he asked.

The bartender pointed to the kiosk. It was outside next to a table with a big umbrella shading it from the sun. The slogan on the umbrella read: 'We don't horse around in the Happy Zebra'.

Harry paid for his drink and crossed the room. As he opened the door he heard the sound he had been waiting for: a high-pitched, tuneless yodelling. He turned round, but he was too late.

'So long, Harry,' the bartender said.

Activity

In the story there are at least fourteen words which have been borrowed from other languages. See if you can work out which words have been borrowed. Can you find out or guess where they might have come from? The answers are at the bottom of this page.

In groups, make a list of all the clues which you could use to help you decide where a word might have come from. Think about words which have strong associations with a particular country, or words which sound or look unusual.

Most of us take language for granted. We use it every day without giving very much thought to where it came from or how it has changed over the years.

However, the more you know about something, the more control you have over it. This is certainly true of language. The greater your knowledge about language, the more effectively you will be able to use it.

Like the magpie that seizes bright objects and brings them back to its nest, the English language is constantly 'stealing' words from other languages as they take the fancy of English-speakers, and making them part of its vocabulary.

This happens for a number of reasons. In some cases we need to find names for things which have only recently been invented, like the video. Quite often people have chosen to use Greek or Latin words as the basis for such new words. The Classical Greek and Latin cultures laid much of the foundation of our modern civilisation. These languages were associated with learning and new ideas and seemed, therefore, a good source of names for new inventions.

For example, 'telephone' comes from two Greek words *tele*, meaning 'from far away', and *phone* meaning 'voice' or 'sound'. So a telephone is a device for making or hearing sounds from far away.

Activity

In pairs, make a list of ten inventions from the last hundred years. Use a large dictionary to find out how many of these have names which come from Latin or Greek.

Answers to So long, Harry

zebra (Bantu), *vodka* (Russian), *sherbet* (Arabic), *dungarees* (Hindi), *anorak* (Inuit), *ukulele* (Hawaiian), *yodel* (German), *opera* (Italian), *tomato* (Mexican Nahuatl), *kiosk* (Persian), *umbrella* (Italian), *slogan* (Gaelic), *medium* (Latin), *thug* (Hindi), *bamboo* (Malay), *hamburger* (German).

Every word tells a story

A word like 'telephone' was introduced suddenly into the English language. It was made up specially because an invention needed a name. Other words have come into the language more slowly and gradually. To understand more about words, it helps to know when they came into the language and where they came from.

500 BC – AD 1066

When the Celts arrived in the British Isles, they brought their language, Celtic, with them. Many places in Britain still have the names that were given to them by the Celts. Look for names ending in 'combe' or 'comb', such as Ilfracombe in Devon or Winchcomb in Gloucestershire. *Cumb* was the Celtic word for a deep valley. (*Cwm* is still used in Welsh with this meaning.)

By the time the Romans invaded in 55 BC, a number of different Celtic languages were being spoken in the British Isles. Latin, which was spoken by the Romans, existed side by side with the Celtic languages for more than four hundred years.

The Romans built military camps in various parts of Britain. Many of the towns which grew up around those camps still have the Latin word for camp, *castra*, in their names. In many cases this has been changed to 'chester' or 'cester'.

Some Latin words also found their way into the English language at this time. For example, 'cup', 'belt', 'street', 'plant', 'purse' and 'fever' are all English versions of Latin words from this time.

By AD 1000 several new groups of people had invaded the British Isles. The best known of the invaders were the Angles and the Saxons. East Anglia, Sussex (the South Saxon kingdom) and Essex (the East Saxon kingdom) are some of the areas named after them. The word 'England' comes from 'Englaland' or 'Anglaland', the land of the Angles. Nearly half of the words we use today come from Old English (or Anglo-Saxon), the language spoken by the Angles and the Saxons.

The battle of the words

After 1066

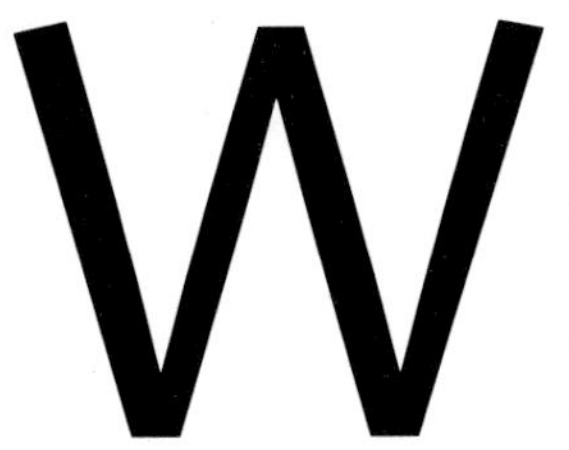

We have already seen that Norman French was not immediately adopted by everyone after the invasion in 1066. Like the Romans before them, the Normans met resistance. It is perhaps not surprising that many of the new words that came into the language at this time were to do with power, the government and the army. These were the areas in which the new rulers could insist that their language was used. Words from this time include 'parliament', 'tax', 'mayor', 'minister' and 'soldier'.

In many cases, new words were adopted alongside those already in use. This explains why there are so many words in English which are very close to each other in meaning.

Examples of other words which have survived from this period are:

Old Norman		**Anglo-Saxon**	
pork	donation	swine	gift
liberty	reception	freedom	welcome

Can I borrow your word?

Borrowing is a two-way process. Some words we commonly use in English have come from French, like *discothèque, rendezvous* or *camouflage*. On the other hand, if you go to France today, you may see signs for *le camping* or hear people talking about *le weekend*.

Investigate

Can you find any other words that we use today which were borrowed from French? One way of doing this is to use a French textbook. You could also pick out words which you recognise from conversations, newspaper extracts and vocabulary lists.

Not all French words which look like English words have the same meaning. For example, the word *informations* in French means 'news', not 'information'. We call words like these 'false friends'. Find out the meanings of these false friends: *actuel, car, prune, sympathique.*

Hot off the press

If you had travelled around the British Isles in the fifteenth century, you would have heard what sounded like a number of different languages being used. Some of these were fairly similar to each other. Others were very different.

Up to this period, most of the major changes in the English language had occurred as a result of invasions. The next major change came about as a result of an invention – the printing press.

The first printing press in England was set up by William Caxton in London in 1476. Soon after this he began printing books.

Caxton was immediately faced with a number of problems. Before this time written English was relatively uncommon. Few people knew how to read and write. Printing was to change that dramatically, but first printers had to make decisions about how to print the words they used. There was no standard version of English in use throughout the country, so in many cases more than one spelling existed for the same word. Caxton had to decide which spellings to use.

This painting by Daniel Maclise (1806–70) shows Edward IV visiting William Caxton's printing shop, sometime during the fifteenth century.

A testing time for spelling

Modern English is a difficult language to spell. You may have wondered how it is that certain spellings are 'correct' today, while others are wrong. Many people assume that somehow, on one particular day, everyone suddenly knew how words should be spelled. This is not the case.

The spellings we have today are a result of many strange accidents. Some words have changed their spelling over a long period. Many changes were introduced, at about this time, by printers who were faced with the same word spelled in many different ways and had to settle for one version. Sometimes decisions were taken purely for the printer's convenience. For example, letters were sometimes added or taken off words so that they would fit onto a line.

One of the problems Caxton faced was that the same word in English can be pronounced differently in different places. As a result, some words came to be spelled differently in different parts of the country because they were pronounced differently.

Activity

Look at these two sets of words:

door	four	core	jaw
know	though	toe	so

Do you pronounce the words in each group to rhyme? If it was up to you, how would you spell each word? Would other people be able to read them? Can you think of other words with the same or similar sounds which are spelled differently?

For Caxton, things were even more complicated. He had spent most of his life in Holland, then moved to Kent, and then set up his press in London, where the form of English he would have encountered was the East Midland one. His spelling of the word 'right' shows this very clearly.

The words 'right' and 'write' are now pronounced the same, but in fifteenth-century London they were pronounced, and therefore spelled, differently. 'Right' was spelled 'richt'. The 'ch' would probably have been pronounced like the 'ch' in 'loch'. In Holland many words with 'h' in them are spelled with 'gh'. Caxton therefore chose to spell it as 'right'.

The need for punctuation

You have already seen how the first printers had to make decisions about the way certain words were spelled. They also had to decide how written English should be presented so that it could be understood on the page. As a result of their decisions, **punctuation** was invented. Punctuation is the way in which we divide up groups of words from each other so that they can easily be read. Various punctuation marks are used.

The most important marks you need to know are:

- **.** A full stop. Used to show that a sentence has ended. (See page 100 for more about sentences.)
- **!** A kind of full stop called an exclamation mark. Used to mark warnings, shouts, or expressions of feeling, such as: 'Look out!', or 'I hate you!'.
- **?** Another kind of full stop called a question mark. Used at the end of questions, such as: 'Have you got the time?' or 'Cup of coffee?'.
- **,** A comma. Used to divide parts of sentences such as the items in a list. For example: 'Give me apples, oranges, pears and bananas'. Or where one part of a sentence can clearly be separated from the rest. For example: 'January, as everyone knows, is the first month of the year'.
- **;** A semi-colon. Used to join parts of a sentence which are closely related. For example: 'He looked up; it was too late; the car's headlights were rushing towards him'.
- **:** A colon. Used to introduce a list. For example: 'There are three things to remember: first, jump out of the plane; second, count to ten; third, pull the rip-cord'.
- **" ,** Speech marks or quotation marks. Normally used in dialogue at the beginning and end of what someone says.

English is a very complicated language and, because of the way in which it developed, it is often difficult to set out many hard and fast 'rules'. Because punctuation marks were standardised by printers, it is easier to give clear guidance about their use than about other aspects of the English language. For example, although you will see different types of speech marks in books and newspapers, these three 'rules' do normally apply:

1 Use speech marks at the beginning and end of what is said.
2 Start a new line for each new speaker.
3 Before the " at the end of speech, use either a **.** or a **,** or a **?** or an **!**.

UPPER and lower case

Printers also introduced small and capital letters; previously a distinction between the two was not always made. In the early days of printing, before word processors were invented, printers arranged lines of print by putting pieces of metal, each with a different letter on the end, into a box. Ink was then applied, and the page was printed when the metal letters touched a sheet of paper. The metal letters were stored in two sets of boxes, or 'cases', capitals on the top shelf, small letters on the bottom one. As a result, printers and some writers still use the term 'upper case' to describe capitals and 'lower case' for small letters.

A printer setting lines of type.

Punctuation can be dangerous

Activity

Read this newspaper article about a comma.

What do you think Mrs Penfold meant to say? How does the comma change the meaning of her words? Was it just the comma that caused the confusion or was there another reason?

COMMA LOST NURSE JOB

A comma cost a nurse, Mrs Angela Penfold, her job, an industrial tribunal ruled yesterday.

Mrs Penfold, aged 50, wrote to her health authority in Torbay, Devon to complain about her senior nurse at a health centre in Bovey Tracey.

She said in her letter: 'I have come to the opinion Mrs Pepperell is out to make my life hell, so I give in my notice.' Because of the unintended comma, the health authority took the letter to be her resignation.

When the authority later refused to allow Mrs Penfold to withdraw the letter, it was effectively sacking her, the tribunal ruled.

The tribunal adjourned a hearing of unfair dismissal on Mrs Penfold of Fore Street, Torquay.

A statement which can have two meanings, like the one Mrs Penfold made, is called an **ambiguous** statement. An ambiguity is a vagueness or confusion about meaning. For example, the sentence below can have two possible meanings. Can you say what they are? How could you use punctuation to make clear what the sentence means?

A few experts I know would disagree with you.

Learning to punctuate

The better you are at punctuating your work, the easier it will be for people to understand what you have written.

Using printers' marks

In Caxton's day, the printer turned what the author had written into neat text and printed it as well. These days, the printer expects to receive a neat text ready for printing from the typesetter. It is the typesetter's job to make sure that the author's text is correct and in good order. To do this, typesetters use certain signs and marks called 'proof correction symbols'.

Activity

Look at the sentence:  it's vanisshed into Thin air 

Instruction	Textual mark	Marginal mark
Delete	/ through character(s) or ⊢⊣ through words	₰
Delete and close up	/ through character(s) or ⊟	₰ (with close-up marks)
Insert in text the matter indicated in the margin	⋏	New matter followed by ⋏
Substitute or insert full stop or decimal point	/ through character or ⋏	⊙
Substitute or insert comma, semicolon, colon, etc.	/ through character or ⋏	,/ ;/ ⊙/ (/)/
Set in or change to capital letters	═══ under character(s)	≡
Change capital letters to lower-case letters	Encircle character(s)	≠
Close up. Delete space between characters or words	⁀‿ linking characters e.g. a⁀scribe	⁀‿
Insert space between characters	| between characters	Y Give the size of the space when necessary

Now study these proof correction symbols. Can you decide what mistakes they indicate that the writer of the sentence has made? How *should* the sentence be written?

Swap a piece of your writing which you are in the process of drafting with that of a partner. Read through your partner's piece and use the proof correction symbols to correct any mistakes you find. When you have finished, swap back and see how many mistakes you noticed in each other's work.

Investigate

Borrow a selection of books from your school library. Select a page from each one and study them closely. Apart from the actual words, do the pages look the same in any way? In pairs, make a list of any differences you find. Use the words given below to help you. (Look up the meaning of any you do not know.)

style of typeface
size of typeface
space left after punctuation
type of speech marks
indentation

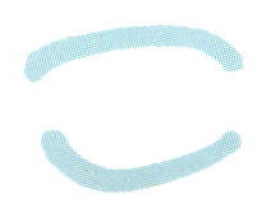

The extraordinary power of Shakespeare

Shakespeare was a legend in his own lifetime, and he has made a lasting impact on the English language. Thousands of ordinary people flocked to see his plays, which were published for the first time soon after his death.

Today, you may think of the theatre as a place where few people go, but four hundred years ago, it was as powerful as television is now.

Look at this story. All the words in **bold type** are expressions directly taken from Shakespeare's plays.

'It's **vanished into thin air**!'

'You mean you've lost it.'

'No, it's just disappeared.'

'Well, it's **high-time** it was returned.'

'Look, the **game is up**. For goodness sake, can't you just tell me the truth?'

'Why won't you believe me? **The long and short of it** is that it's gone, vanished, disappeared, been nicked, okay?'

'Young lady, you are a **blinking idiot** and you leave me with no option but to fine you.'

'But that's not right. Where is your sense of **fair play**? It had **seen better days** anyway. I don't see why I should pay anything, as it is not my fault.'

'No excuses. I'm telling you. Give me the money or I'll ...' The librarian, who was by now extremely red in the face, paused as if he was thinking exactly what he would do to this irritating girl. Jane didn't **budge an inch**. She had always known that her excuse sounded pretty feeble. Summoning up her best annoyed voice, she looked the librarian in the eyes and, before she could stop herself, shouted,

'You **bloody-minded** old fool. I don't care what you say.'

With that she turned on her heels and walked out of the library.

Many of Shakespeare's famous lines, sayings and expressions have found their way into the English language.

Activity

Using a dictionary of quotations, find out which of Shakespeare's plays these expressions have been taken from. You will need to use the dictionary's index effectively to be able to do this. How many of them do you know? Where did you come across them? Can you find out any more famous lines from Shakespeare's plays?

New words

Perhaps Shakespeare's most significant contribution to the development of English was in the new words he introduced into the language. He was especially interested in experimenting with words which came from Latin, which was then in fashion because of a new interest in Classical times. It has been estimated that Shakespeare had a vocabulary of about thirty thousand words.

Activity

The words below all come from Shakespeare's plays. Which are in use today?

Make two lists, one of words which have not survived and one of those in use today.

Many of those which have survived were invented or first used by Shakespeare. Can you give examples of how these words are used today?

multitudinous incarnadine armada emphasis horrid vast demonstrate honorificabilitudinatibus critical compunctious stratagem

The Bible as bestseller

Before 1535, only a few English translations of the Bible existed. Between 1535 and 1568, largely as a result of Henry VIII's decision to leave the Roman Catholic Church and set up his own, there were five new English translations of the Bible. Each one was a bestseller.

Henry VIII's Great Bible.

In 1604, James I asked a special conference of Church leaders to produce a new translation. As a result, the Authorised Version of the Bible was produced. Along with Shakespeare's plays, this and later versions of the Bible have made a huge impact on the English language.

One of the best-known parts of the Bible is the Lord's Prayer. It gives an interesting picture of the way English has changed over the years.

Anglo-Saxon Version
Faeder ure thu the eart on heofonum
si thin nama gehalgod
to-becume thin rice
gewirthe thin wille on eorthan swa swa on heofenum
urne daeghwaemlice hlaf syle us todaeg
and forgyf us ure gyltas
swa swa we forgyfath urum gyltendum
and ne gelaed thu us on costunge
ac alys us of yfele, sothlice.

The Authorised Version (1611)
Our Father which art in heaven
Hallowed be thy name.
Thy kingdom come.
Thy will be done in earth,
as it is in heaven.
Give us this day our daily bread.
And forgive us our debts,
As we forgive our debtors.
And lead us not into temptation,
But deliver us from evil:
For thine is the kingdom, and the power,
and the glory, for ever.

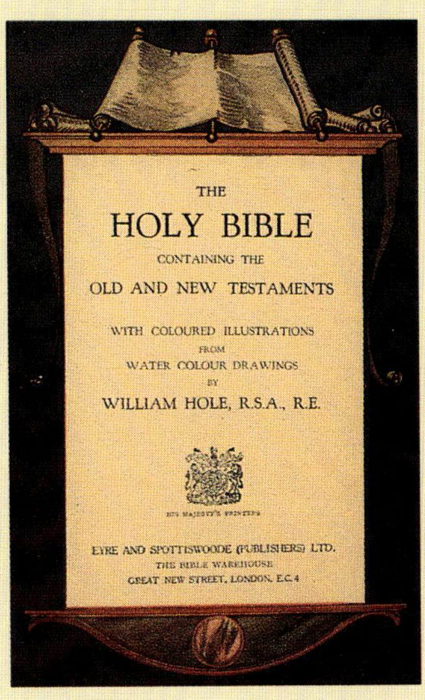
THE
HOLY BIBLE
CONTAINING THE
OLD AND NEW TESTAMENTS
WITH COLOURED ILLUSTRATIONS
FROM
WATER COLOUR DRAWINGS
BY
WILLIAM HOLE, R.S.A., R.E.

EYRE AND SPOTTISWOODE (PUBLISHERS) LTD.
THE BIBLE WAREHOUSE
GREAT NEW STREET, LONDON, E.C.4

The New English Bible (1959)
Our Father in heaven,
thy name be hallowed;
thy kingdom come,
thy will be done,
on earth as in heaven.
Give us today our daily bread.
Forgive us the wrong we have done,
as we have forgiven those who have wronged us.
And do not bring us to the test,
but save us from the evil one.

The Revised English Bible (1989)
Our Father in heaven,
may your name be hallowed;
your kingdom come,
your will be done,
on earth as in heaven.
Give us today our daily bread
Forgive us the wrong we have done,
as we have forgiven those who have wronged us.
And do not put us to the test,
but save us from the evil one.

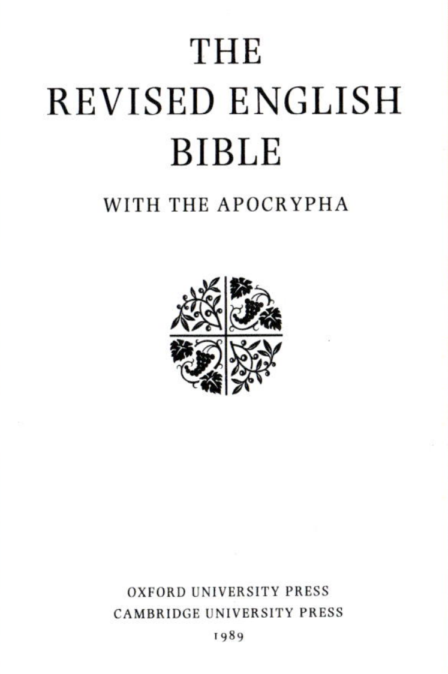
THE
REVISED ENGLISH
BIBLE
WITH THE APOCRYPHA

OXFORD UNIVERSITY PRESS
CAMBRIDGE UNIVERSITY PRESS
1989

Activity

What kind of changes can you see? Read each version aloud. Which one do you think sounds the most effective?

The Bible and English

An **archaism** is a word or form of a word which was used in the past but which has died out. For example, 'thy' is an archaism in the New English Bible version, because it had died out of normal use more than a hundred years earlier, being replaced by 'your'. Can you see any archaisms in the most recent version, taken from the Revised English Bible?

Investigate

Open the page of any modern Bible. How many words can you find which are archaisms? What effect do you think the Bible achieves by 'hanging on' to words which many people have stopped using?

How grammar got a bad name

There are many different views of grammar and many misunderstandings about it.

You will already have begun to see how the English language has gone through a process of continual change. There are many ways of describing how such a complicated living language works. One word often used for describing the structure of a language at any point in time is **grammar**.

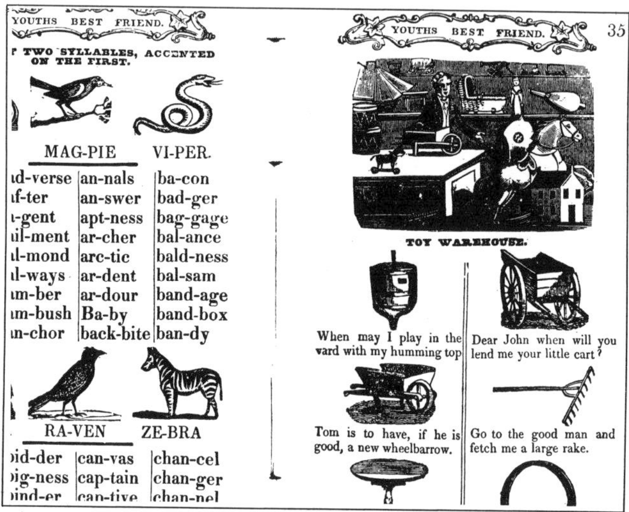
YOUTHS BEST FRIEND.

TWO SYLLABLES, ACCENTED ON THE FIRST.

MAG-PIE VI-PER.

ad-verse	an-nals	ba-con
af-ter	an-swer	bad-ger
a-gent	apt-ness	bag-gage
ail-ment	ar-cher	bal-ance
al-mond	arc-tic	bald-ness
al-ways	ar-dent	bal-sam
am-ber	ar-dour	band-age
am-bush	Ba-by	band-box
an-chor	back-bite	ban-dy

RA-VEN ZE-BRA

bid-der	can-vas	chan-cel
big-ness	cap-tain	chan-ger
bind-er	cap-tive	chan-nel

YOUTHS BEST FRIEND. 35

TOY WAREHOUSE.

When may I play in the yard with my humming top

Dear John when will you lend me your little cart?

Tom is to have, if he is good, a new wheelbarrow.

Go to the good man and fetch me a large rake.

A Briefe note of the Moodes according to the English tongue.

These are all pages taken from early grammar books.

Greek and Latin lead the way

In the sixteenth century, the word **grammar** started to be used. It originally came from a Greek word and meant 'to do with letters'. It was mainly used to describe the structure of the Latin language, rather than English. (Latin was still read by many educated people.)

A
PERFECT
SVRVEY OF THE
ENGLISH TONGVE,
TAKEN ACCORDING TO
THE VSE AND ANALOGIE
of the LATINE.

And ſerueth for the more plaine expoſition of the Grammaticall Rules and Precepts, collected by LILLIE, and for the more certaine Tranſlation of the *Engliſh* tongue into *Latine*.

Together with ſundry good demonſtrations, by way of Sentences in either tongue.

Written and collected by *Io: Hewes*, Maſter of Arts.

Principijs cognitis, multo faciliùs extrema intelligentur.
Cic. *pro* Cluentio:

LONDON.
Printed by *Edw: All-de*, for *William Garret*.
1624.

A new kind of school, called a 'grammar school', was created specially to teach children about Latin and its grammar. It was thought that this was the best kind of education for them.

In the eighteenth century, a number of thinkers and writers began to take a new interest in language (see pages 32–3). They assumed that English was like Latin and should, therefore, obey the same rules. Many school grammar books were based on ideas developed at this time and did not change very much until well into the twentieth century.

However, there are a great many differences between English and Latin and many of the rules suggested by grammarians simply did not accurately describe the way English was used. For example, one such rule stated that we should say 'it is I' and not 'it is me', just because Latin uses its word for 'I' rather than its word for 'me' in this sentence.

Very few people stick to this 'rule', because it isn't a rule which comes naturally to English-speakers. There are other similar 'rules' which are broken more often than they are observed. As a result, it is not uncommon to hear complaints that English is degenerating, or that people don't know how to speak or write properly nowadays. The idea that unless people stick to rules, they are using English badly is called the **prescriptive** view of language.

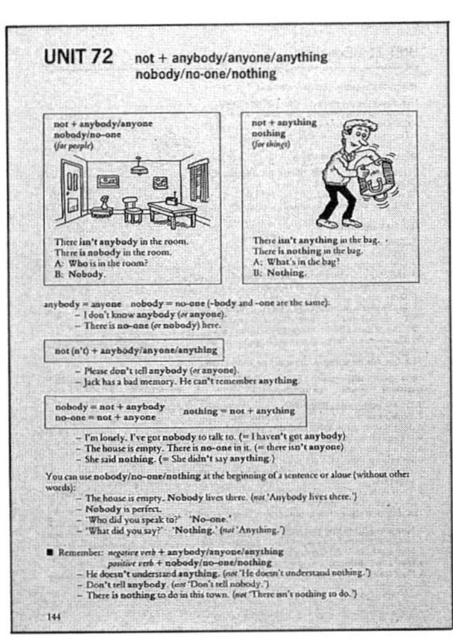

UNIT 72 not + anybody/anyone/anything
nobody/no-one/nothing

not + anybody/anyone
nobody/no-one
(for people)

There **isn't anybody** in the room.
There is **nobody** in the room.
A: Who is in the room?
B: **Nobody**.

not + anything
nothing
(for things)

There **isn't anything** in the bag.
There is **nothing** in the bag.
A: What's in the bag?
B: **Nothing**.

anybody = anyone **nobody = no-one** (-**body** and -**one** are the same):
- I don't know **anybody** (*or* **anyone**).
- There is **no-one** (*or* **nobody**) here.

not (n't) + anybody/anyone/anything

- Please don't tell **anybody** (*or* **anyone**).
- Jack has a bad memory. He can't remember **anything**.

nobody = not + anybody
no-one = not + anyone
nothing = not + anything

- I'm lonely. I've got **nobody** to talk to. (= I **haven't** got **anybody**)
- The house is empty. There is **no-one** in it. (= there **isn't anyone**)
- She said **nothing**. (= She **didn't** say **anything**.)

You can use **nobody/no-one/nothing** at the beginning of a sentence or alone (without other words):
- The house is empty. **Nobody** lives there. (*not* 'Anybody lives there.')
- **Nobody** is perfect.
- 'Who did you speak to?' '**No-one**.'
- 'What did you say?' '**Nothing**.' (*not* 'Anything.')

■ Remember: *negative verb* + **anybody/anyone/anything**
positive verb + **nobody/no-one/nothing**
- He **doesn't** understand **anything**. (*not* 'He doesn't understand nothing.')
- **Don't** tell **anybody**. (*not* 'Don't tell nobody.')
- There **is nothing** to do in this town. (*not* 'There isn't nothing to do.')

144

More recently, people who study language have taken the view that it is more helpful if rules describe the way language is used, rather than trying to dictate the way it is used. This view is called the **descriptive** view of language.

Language naturally has rules, otherwise no one would be able to understand anyone else, and a knowledge of the way language works is essential for anyone who wishes to use it effectively. However, many people think of grammar simply as a set of labels (for example, words like 'noun' and 'verb'), which need to be learned. In fact, knowledge about language involves a lot more than this.

Different ways of knowing about language

It is important to realise that knowledge about language takes many forms. It covers alphabets and books, sentences and stories, television and myths, and lots more.

When we use the word 'grammar' we tend to mean the way in which sentences are put together. But this is not a simple matter. There are a number of aspects involved. We use the terms **syntax**, **morphology** and **parts of speech** to describe three ways of looking at words in a sentence.

GRAMMAR

Syntax
the order of words

For example:
'grammar is complicated' (not 'complicated grammar is').

Morphology
the way individual words change

For example:
run → ran → running.

Parts of speech
the way different types of word are classified

For example:
nouns, verbs adjectives, and so on.

Being able to put words together into a sentence that others will be able to understand is something that nearly all of us learn naturally as children and continue to develop as we grow older.

For example, we learn about syntax or word order, and this seems very obvious to us. However, it is important to remember that in other languages word order can be quite different to that in English.

We may well also understand that there are different kinds of words, that 'ball' and 'table' are different to 'looking' and 'danced'. Some people might not know that 'ball' and 'table' are nouns, whereas 'looking' and 'danced' are verbs. Nevertheless, most of us could think of a group of words that are of the same type as 'ball', and another group that are of the same type as 'counting'.

Similarly, we learn quite early on how words change according to their function. Most people would see the mistake in morphology here:

'I rided my bicycle down the street'

although a very young child, just beginning to talk in sentences, might not.

We learn this kind of grammar by experience from our language community, and only occasionally do we have to be taught. This experience comes mainly through speaking.

Are there any rules?

Activity

Look at these sentences spoken by young children:

1 I can see three womans.

2 She's taked my book.

3 Can you louden the radio, please?

Clearly they are in English and not in a foreign language, but how do you know? What is it that makes you so sure?

- Do you think any of them have mistakes in them? What are they?
- Why do you think children speak in this way?
- Does it make you think that there are some rules in English?

Imagine that you are trying to produce some simple rules for a book about English grammar. Can you use each sentence to make up a rule about how the language should not be used?

Investigate

Collect other examples of the mistakes young children make (for example, 'mans'). Don't write down the ones where they are just pronouncing words wrongly.

Correct each mistake and then try to work out what rule the child is applying in making the mistake. Can you give examples (for instance, 'boys') of when the child would be correct in applying the rule?

A little knowledge is a dangerous thing

Parts of speech

When learning about English, it is important to realise that different kinds of words behave in different ways. English words are normally divided up into eight different kinds, called **parts of speech**. Parts of speech are rather like the major parts of a car. You don't need to know what a carburettor is to be able to drive a car. But if you want to improve the running of a car, it is helpful to be able to describe a certain part of your car's engine which seems not to be working. In the same way, if you want to talk about your writing, it will help you to know about different parts of speech.

The three major parts of speech are **nouns**, **verbs** and **adjectives**.

Nouns	It seems sensible to start with nouns because it is likely that they were the first kind of words to be used as language developed. Nouns are words like *tree, bed, dog, girl* and *mouse* – the names of people and things. Nouns normally have a plural and singular form, for example: *bed/beds* and *mouse/mice*.
Verbs	Verbs, like *go, help, be, sleep, fight* and *talk*,are used to mean activities. These can be happening at different times, and because of this, verbs have several different forms, for example: *I had gone, I went, I have gone, I go, I am going, I shall go, I shall have gone.*
Adjectives	Adjectives tend to go with nouns. They add description, for example: *hot, cold, happy* and *red*. 'A hot day' is an example of an adjective (hot) telling you more about a noun (day).

Even the most precise definitions of these parts of speech can sometimes be unhelpful or lead to confusion.

Answers to questions about collective nouns:
a pack **c** herd **e** shoal **g** pride **i** troop
b nest **d** murder **f** smack **h** plague **j** knot

Read this poem by Mike Rosen.

Poem

The teacher said:
A noun is a naming word.
What is a naming word
in the sentence
'He named the ship,
Lusitania'?
'Named' said George.
'WRONG – it's ship'.

The teacher said:
A verb is a doing word.
What is the doing word
in the sentence
'I like doing homework'?
'Doing' said George.
'WRONG – it's like.'

The teacher said:
An adjective is a describing
word.
What is the describing word
in the sentence
'Describing sunsets is boring'?
'Describing' said George.
'WRONG – it's boring.'
'I know it is,' said George.

Activity

Choose the sentence in each verse which defined the part of speech. Why is it confusing? Give an example to make your point.

You can begin to recognise certain characteristics of these parts of speech and the particular situations in which they are used.

Try these three examples:

a Make a list of what you would like for your next birthday. What kinds of words are these?

b Close your eyes and describe a member of your family. What are the words which make the features of your person special (for example, long, brown hair)?

c Imagine you are commentating on a sports match or describing a car accident. Words to do with kicking, running, hitting, and so on are which part of speech?

Examples of the five other parts of speech are:

> adverbs (add description to verbs), for example: *quickly, quietly, fast, slowly*
> pronouns (a special kind of noun), for example: *she, he, it, they*
> prepositions, for example: *in, under, on, with*
> conjunctions, for example: *and, because, but*
> interjections, for example: *hi!, ouch!, help!*

Investigate

There is a special kind of noun called a **collective noun** which is used to describe a group, like a *flock* of sheep or a *litter* of kittens.

Find out what the collective nouns are for:

a wolves **c** cattle **e** fish **g** lions **i** monkeys
b vipers **d** crows **f** jellyfish **h** locusts **j** toads

(The answers are on page 30.)

Look it up in the dictionary

dictionary *n.* a book which lists and explains the words of a language or the words and topics of a particular subject, usually in alphabetical order.

lexicography *leks-i-kog-ra-fi, n.* the writing and compiling of dictionaries – *n.* **lexicographer**.

The most commonly used reference book is the **dictionary**. It is used to settle disputes about the spelling of words, to find out meanings of words and to check which is the right word for a particular occasion.

People say 'the' dictionary, as if there were only one. In fact, there are hundreds of dictionaries and, surprisingly, they are sometimes very different. The people who compile them are called **lexicographers**. Their job involves sorting through the vast number of words that make up the English language. They have to decide what to include, what to leave out and what each word means.

This is an immense task. The *Oxford English Dictionary* lists about five hundred thousand words and the lexicographers who work on it are still considering a further half million technical and scientific terms.

The first dictionary of English was written by Dr Samuel Johnson (1709–84) in 1755. He thought that the language of the time was in a mess and that unless something was done to fix standards, people would soon be unable to talk or write to each other. A word used by one person might mean something quite different to someone else. He believed that it was a lexicographer's duty to correct people when they 'used words wrongly'.

If Dr Johnson were alive now, he might well be appalled to find that the word 'wicked' is being used to mean 'very good'. For him 'wicked' meant 'evil'. He would never have bought a record with the title *Bad*. When he heard something described as 'cool', he would doubtless have assumed that it was not hot.

Dr Johnson.

Most modern dictionaries take a different view to Dr Johnson's. They attempt to describe the ways in which words are actually used, not the ways in which the lexicographer thinks they ought to be used. For example, a descriptive dictionary might give a number of meanings for the word 'cool', including 'fashionable', 'stylish' and even 'enjoyable'. A good dictionary will help the reader with information about whether certain words are regarded as slang or as offensive.

A major change in the way in which lexicographers looked at language took place in 1879, when James Murray (1837–1915) began work on the *Oxford English Dictionary*. He defined words by giving their earliest use and then tracing the history of their meaning through the ages up to the current time.

His way of looking at words was rather like the picture we have of an iceberg. Most of the meanings of words are hidden in the past, just as the bulk of an iceberg is below the water-line. But the current meaning of a word often depends, like the tip of the iceberg, on what lies beneath the surface.

One example of this is the word 'boot'. Originally 'boot' meant something worn on the foot, as it still does today. But in the seventeenth century, it was also used to mean the step on a coach, where a person placed their boot when getting into the coach. Later, it came to mean the space at the side of the step where an attendant stood. Later still, it was used to describe the rear of the coach which was set aside for the servant. Finally, it was used for the space for luggage in a motor car.

Murray's attitude influenced other lexicographers. It led to the view of language held by many people today, namely that words change their meaning according to the way they are used. They mean different things at different times and in different places.

Murray had seriously underestimated the job of compiling a dictionary which was to include every word in the English language. By 1884, five years after starting the project, he had only reached the word 'ant'. By the time the complete *Oxford English Dictionary* finally appeared in 1928, Murray had been dead for many years.

Activity

Get hold of as many English dictionaries as you can. Look up 'boot' in each one. How many different definitions of 'boot' are there? How are they the same and how do they differ? What different signs or abbreviations are used? Choose ten other words from a book you are reading at the moment. Look up their definitions. Are they different in any way?

From Johnson to Webster

When Samuel Johnson started work on his famous dictionary, he was assisted by five clerks scribbling furiously in a small attic room. James Murray called on the help of clergymen throughout the world, who worked as volunteers, sending him information about any unusual words they encountered.

Nowadays lexicographers rely heavily on modern technology. The lexicographers currently working on the *Oxford English Dictionary* have their own computer with a huge database containing millions of words.

They also have information provided by a team of people who read books and magazines written in English from all over the world. The readers regularly send in **citations**, which are examples of new words or words being used in a different way. The citations are written on cards which are kept in an enormous filing system.

With the help of all this information, the lexicographers are able to make a list of the **attributes** of a word. By this they mean everything that we think of when we come across that word. For example, a list for the word 'dog' might include the information that a dog is an animal, that it has four legs, eats meat, has often been called 'a man's best friend', and so on. From this list, the lexicographers will select those details that are significant and those which distinguish the word 'dog' from other words.

They can use the same methods to make decisions about spelling. American spellings are becoming much more widely used in Britain and lexicographers have to decide whether, in some cases, the American spelling has become standard. For example, the

All of these people are involved in choosing the words for a new dictionary.

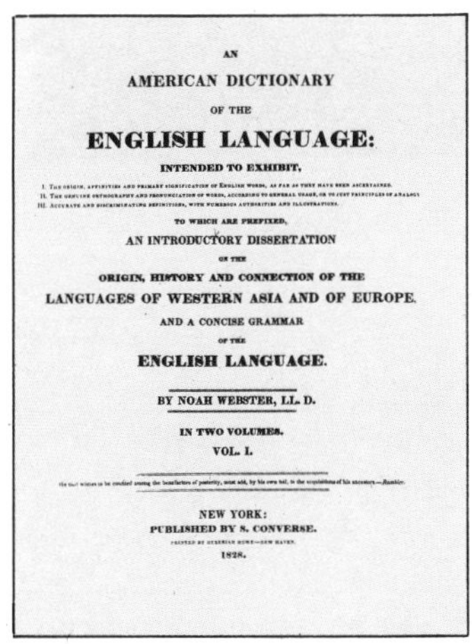

AN
AMERICAN DICTIONARY
OF THE
ENGLISH LANGUAGE:
INTENDED TO EXHIBIT,

TO WHICH ARE PREFIXED,
AN INTRODUCTORY DISSERTATION
ON THE
ORIGIN, HISTORY AND CONNECTION OF THE
LANGUAGES OF WESTERN ASIA AND OF EUROPE.
AND A CONCISE GRAMMAR
OF THE
ENGLISH LANGUAGE.

BY NOAH WEBSTER, LL. D.

IN TWO VOLUMES.
VOL. I.

NEW YORK:
PUBLISHED BY S. CONVERSE.
1828.

American spelling 'jail' is now more commonly used than the British 'gaol'.

Quite often American English words go back to that period before independence was gained from Britain. If we look more closely we may find that it is British English that has changed. An example of this is the word 'faucet', which is used by Americans where the British would say 'tap'. In fact, 'faucet' is a much earlier word and not, as some people might think, a modern term.

The first proper dictionary of American English was compiled by Noah Webster (1758–1843) in 1828. He was particularly keen to show that American English was different from the English spoken in Britain.

Lexicographers today have to take into account the influence of American English. When we turn on the television, we often see the words 'center' and 'color' instead of the more familiar 'centre' and 'colour'.

Activity

How many words do you regularly use which you think might come from America? Make a list of them and compare your list with a friend's.

Investigate

Select an American television show. Make a note of all the words you hear which are not commonly used by you, your friends or your family. Compare them with other lists made by people in your class. Agree on a list of the ten most commonly used American English words from the television programmes you have watched. Which words would you have used instead?

Where else do you come across American English? Find out how many different ways, apart from in novels, in which you come across American English.

Atlantic crossing

ne of the obvious ways in which American English becomes used across the world is through American novels by writers like Betsy Byars, Judy Blume, Alan Cormier, S. E. Hinton, Paul Zindel and Paula Danziger.

Activity

Read this extract from the beginning of *Can you sue your parents for malpractice?* by Paula Danziger. As you read, see how many American English words or spellings you notice.

'Lauren, why was the skeleton afraid to cross the road?'

I pretend I don't hear Linda.

She keeps talking anyway. 'Because he had no guts.'

It's hard coping with a ten-year-old sister who wants to be a stand-up comic and treats the family as a captive audience for all her routines. It's especially hard while I'm trying to get over a broken heart.

'Look,' I say, 'would you please go away? I've got to study my Spanish. There's a quiz tomorrow. I flunked the last one and I've got to get an A on this one, or else.'

'Just one more. Please, Lauren, then I promise to go.'

I wonder how many other fourteen-year-olds in the world have to deal with a younger sister determined to take her show on the road. It's not that I don't like her, it's just that my mind's on other things right now.

She looks so hurt.

I say, 'Oh, OK. But just one more. I really do have to study. You'll see what it's like when you get to ninth grade and have to worry about grades to get into college.'

She grins. 'Did you hear the one about the rodent who

Activity

How did you decide which words or spelling patterns were American English? How many of them are you familiar with? How many do you use? Make a list of American English words with their British English meanings.

Investigate

How many books by American authors are there in your class or school library? Read the rest of Paula Danziger's book or choose another American novel to read.

almost drowned and his brother had to give him mouse to mouse resuscitation?'

'Out,' I yell. 'Enough is enough.'

Linda goes, 'Da da di da da da,' and tap dances out of the room.

I laugh at the dumb joke after she leaves, and shake my head. She's got a right to her dreams. It's just that my mind's on other things right now.

My special elective class, 'Law for Children and Young People' is about to start. And I definitely have lots of questions. It's a good thing the school started it just in time for everything I have to ask. The first one's going to be 'What are the grounds for justifiable homicide?' Can I kill off one or more of the following: an older sister who gets her own room and ends up with all the beauty genes in the family? A mother who lives in a fantasy world always dreaming about winning the lottery or some big prize so we can all live happily ever after? A mother who's always writing letters and going to try-outs for quiz shows? A father who constantly complains about how hard it is to sell insurance and to support a family in this day and age? Sandy Linwood, who stole my boy-friend because she goes further than I do?

two THIS IS THE SIX O'CLOCK NEWS

Starting Point

Jap Planes Raid Manila

Congress Declares War

One of our warships is sunk

12 EVIL MEN TO HANG

Murder Of A Nation

Fury In South Africa

KENNEDY SLAIN ON DALLAS SREET

Few people can entirely avoid being influenced by newspapers. Their headlines and articles are read by millions. The language they use has undoubtedly influenced the development of English and will continue to do so. Newspapers deal daily with a huge range of subjects – from bad news of war or disaster, to news of parliament or business affairs, to coverage of sports and arts events – all of which have their own specialist vocabulary.

Investigate

Look at a selection of local and national newspapers. Make a list of all the ways in which you think they use language differently, from the size of the print and the style of headlines they use, to the length of individual words and articles.

The development of mass communication

People have always been interested in new or interesting information. In the Middle Ages, town criers were appointed to tell people about official news. They were a sort of speaking notice-board for people who could not read.

Once printing had been invented, pamphlets and newsletters began to be produced. In 1702, the first daily newspaper, the *Daily Courant*, was published. News about war, royal scandals, celebrities and other current affairs was now widely available for the first time.

Inventions like the telephone, railways, radio and television have led directly to the age of mass communications in which we now live.

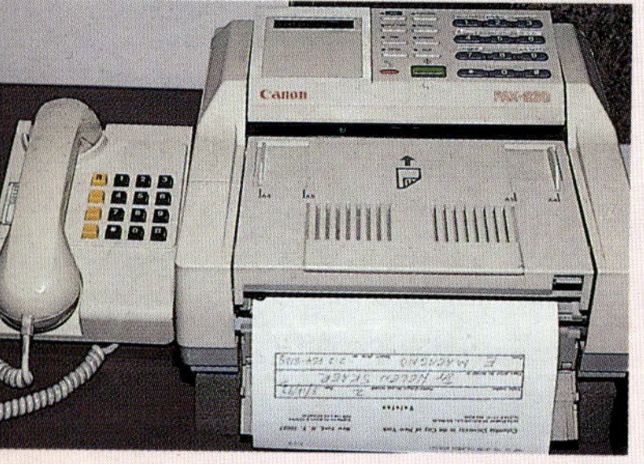

As a result of this, few people are more than twenty-four hours away from national or international news. The language we experience, therefore, is no longer simply the speech of those living in our area or the books which we choose to read. It is no longer possible to 'hide' from new words. Within a matter of a few hours, a particular word may be used all over the world. Can you think of examples of new words which have suddenly become well known?

Activity

Cameramen sometimes have to get into precarious positions to film news stories.

What do you think it would have been like living in a remote village in England two hundred years ago as far as news goes? How would your understanding of the world have been different from yours today?

Look at these statements. Which do you agree with? Which do you disagree with, and why?

- War is the most important news.
- News about Britain is more important than foreign news.
- People want to know about crime for their entertainment.
- People need to know about crime for their protection.
- Everyone has a right to a private life.
- Newspapers use language that is easy to understand.
- Newspapers use language that is confusing.

What are your views?

The wireless arrives

Although some people use the radio more for music than for listening to news, the radio has proved itself to be a powerful **medium** for communication. A medium is any channel or means through which information can be transmitted to the public. Normally we use it in the plural form, **media**, to describe newspapers, radio and television. These kinds of channels are also known as the 'mass media' because of the large numbers of people they can reach.

Radio or 'the wireless', as it was called then, was particularly important during the Second World War. Throughout the war it was people's main source of information about what was going on each day. Radio is especially interesting as far as language is concerned, because there are no pictures or images to accompany the spoken words. The way a person speaks is therefore very important.

This is a small part of a famous speech made by Winston Churchill:

> We have before us an ordeal of the most grievous kind. We have before us many, many long months of struggle and of suffering. You ask, what is our policy? I will say: It is to wage war, by sea, land and air, with all our might and with all the strength that God can give us; to wage war against a monstrous tyranny never surpassed in the dark, lamentable catalogue of human crime. This is our policy. You ask, what is our aim? I can answer in one word: It is victory, victory at all cost, victory in spite of all terror, victory, however long and hard the road may be; for without victory, there is no survival. Let that be realized; no survival for the British Empire, no survival for all that the British Empire has stood for, no survival for the urge and impulse of the ages, that mankind will move forward towards its goal. But I take up my task with buoyancy and hope. I feel sure that our cause will not be suffered to fail among men. At this time I feel entitled to claim the aid of all, and I say, 'Come then, let us go forward together with our united strength.'

Withdrawal from Dunkirk (1940) by Charles Cundall.

Activity

Read the extract aloud. Why do you think Churchill repeats certain groups of words? What effect does it have? What does it make you think or feel?

The power of television

I have a dream

It is now possible, via satellite dishes, to transmit news from the surface of the moon, from the scene of an assassination or from the middle of a war.

However, it is difficult to find out exactly how all this affects us.

Sometimes we can say that a particular speech has helped to change our ideas, such as this speech given by Martin Luther King, Jr., in 1963.

Martin Luther King, Jr.

I have a dream that my four little children will one day live in a nation where they will not be judged by the colour of their skin but by the content of their character.

I have a dream today.

I have a dream that one day the state of Alabama, whose governor's lips are presently dripping with the words of interposition and nullification, will be transformed into a situation where little black boys and black girls will be able to join hands with little white boys and white girls and walk together as sisters and brothers.

I have a dream today.

I have a dream that one day every valley shall be exalted, every hill and mountain shall be made low, the rough places will be made plain, and the crooked places will be made straight, and the glory of the Lord shall be revealed, and all flesh shall see it together.

This is our hope. This is the faith with which I return to the South. With this faith we will be able to hew out of the mountain of despair a stone of hope. With this faith we will be able to transform the jangling discords of our nation into a beautiful symphony of brotherhood. With this faith we will be able to work together, to pray together, to struggle together, to go to jail together, to stand up for freedom together, knowing that we will be free one day.

This will be the day when all of God's children will be able to sing with new meaning 'My country 'tis of thee, sweet land of liberty, of thee I sing. Land where my fathers died, land of the pilgrim's pride, from every mountainside, let freedom ring.'

And if America is to be a great nation this must become true. So let freedom ring from the prodigious hilltops of New Hampshire! Let freedom ring from the mighty mountains of New York!

Let freedom ring from the heightening Alleghenies of Pennsylvania! Let freedom ring from the snowcapped Rockies of Colorado!

Let freedom ring from the curvaceous peaks of California!

But not only that; let freedom ring from the Stone Mountain of Georgia!

Let freedom ring from every hill and mole hill of Mississippi. From every mountainside, let freedom ring.

When we let freedom ring, when we let it ring from every village and every hamlet, from every state and every city, we will be able to speed up that day when all of God's children, black men and white men, Jews and Gentiles, Protestants and Catholics, will be able to join hands and sing in the words of that old Negro spiritual, 'Free at last! Free at last! Thank God almighty, we are free at last!'

Activity

What is Martin Luther King's dream? Which words do you think he has used particularly effectively?

Occasionally we can see exactly how television (or another medium) changes language. On 4 October 1957, the Russians launched a spacecraft called *Sputnik*. As a direct result of the world media coverage of this event, the word 'sputnik' entered the English language overnight and now appears in many dictionaries.

Sputnik.

Harry Enfield.

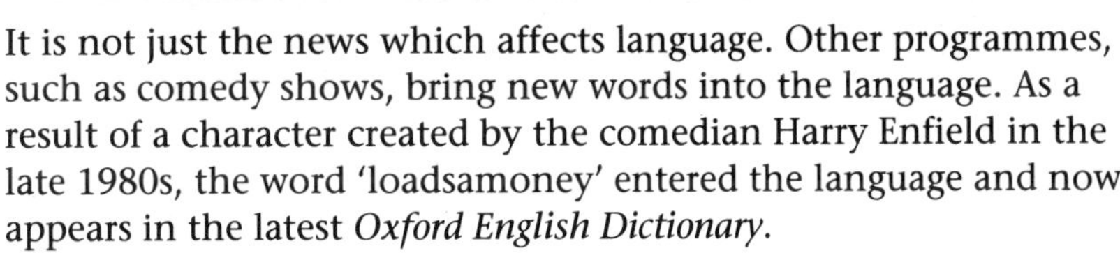

It is not just the news which affects language. Other programmes, such as comedy shows, bring new words into the language. As a result of a character created by the comedian Harry Enfield in the late 1980s, the word 'loadsamoney' entered the language and now appears in the latest *Oxford English Dictionary*.

Investigate

Can you think of any catch-phrases or other expressions which you and your friends use because you heard them on television? Start to keep a record of them.

Television events

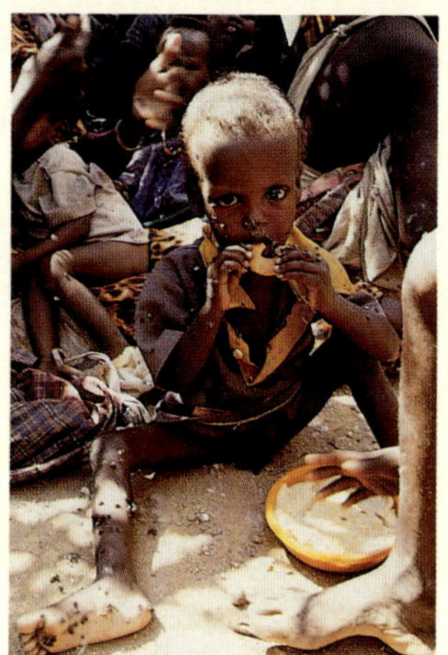

Sometimes a television event can be so influential that its name begins to affect the way we use language.

Bob Geldof, an Irish pop star who was the lead singer with a group called the *Boomtown Rats*, saw a television news report about an appalling famine in Ethiopia. He describes the impact which both the pictures and the words used by the reporter had on him:

> The images played and replayed in my mind. What could I do? I could send money, of course, but that did not seem enough. Did not the sheer scale of the whole thing call for something more? The reporter had used the word 'biblical'. A famine of biblical proportions. There was something terrible about the idea that two thousand years after Christ, in a world of modern technology, something like this could be allowed to happen.

With a number of other pop stars, Geldof made a record in aid of famine relief. The musicians and singers came from a number of other rock bands, so they called their group *Band Aid*, which is also the name of a sticking-plaster used for first aid.

On 13 July 1985, *Band Aid* played live along with a host of other musicians and celebrities. The concert took place simultaneously in London and in Philadelphia in the United States of America. It was watched on television by an estimated two billion people, one-third of the earth's entire population. The concert became known as *Live Aid*.

Activity

A **suffix** is a group of letters added to the end of a word. How many words can you think of which end with the suffix '-aid'?

Television – friend or foe?

Not everybody is happy about the effect television is having on the English language.

The National Viewers' and Listeners' Association, founded by Mary Whitehouse, monitors the way in which it thinks television is affecting the English language. In two recent reports on 'The Debasement of Language', it claimed that the English language is being spoiled by television, particularly through the use of swearing.

In the second of the two reports, Mary Whitehouse said:

> In our first report (May 1991), we revealed that the incidence of bad language on television had more than doubled in the two years between 16 April 1989 and 31 March 1991.
>
> The second report reveals that the incidence of bad language has more than doubled in the first nine months of this year (1991). Swear-words and blasphemous expressions totalled 2,340, an annual rate of 3,120.
>
> We would emphasise that this research covers only films shown after the nine o'clock at night watershed.

Activity

Do you agree with Mary Whitehouse? Working in groups, look at the following statements. Talk together about them and decide which you agree with and which you disagree with.

- There is too much swearing on television.
- More people will swear if there is swearing on television.
- People are not influenced by television.
- If people use bad language, then it should appear on television.

Investigate

In what other ways do you think television might affect language? (You have already seen examples of new words such as 'sputnik' and 'loadsamoney'.)

Stretching out a word

word

Adding letters to the beginning and end of a word has always been one way of creating a new word. Additions such as these are known as prefixes and suffixes. They often have a dash called a hyphen to show where they have been joined to the original word.

A **prefix** is a group of letters added to the beginning of a word, like '**multi**-storey' or '**re**tell'.

A **suffix** is a group of letters added to the end of a word, like 'high**ness**' or 'penni**less**'.

Activity

Look at these words which have been introduced into the English language in the last eighty years. Beside each is the date when it began to be used.
Decide which of the words have suffixes and which prefixes. In each case, decide what the prefix or suffix means. Which of these words do you use? Look up the meaning of any which you do not know. Where do you think they might have come from?

devaluation 1914
beltful 1916
junkie 1923
multipurpose 1935
baddy 1937
biggy 1937
multicultural 1941
gimmickry 1952
non-music 1958
beatnik 1958
sit-in 1960
non-event 1962
noshery 1963
metrication 1965
banditry 1965
mini-skirt 1965
kiss-in 1968
laugh-in 1968
mini-computer 1968

word

Shrinking words

New words can also be formed by shortening existing words. Sometimes these words continue to exist as **abbreviations** (shortened forms); there are thousands of abbreviations in English. Some of these are formed by leaving off part of a word. For example, people sometimes say 'glam' instead of 'glamorous'. Shortened forms like this can be made from the beginning, the middle or the end of an existing word, and the spelling of the word may be changed slightly.

Shortened forms of words often become accepted as new words in their own right. For example, 'phone' began as a shortened version of 'telephone', 'fridge' comes from 'refrigerator' and 'bus' comes from 'omnibus'. Although we still often use the complete form of the first two of these examples, hardly anyone talks about catching an 'omnibus' these days.

We also use **contractions**, particularly for titles like 'Dr' and 'Mr'. In these two cases, only the first and last letters of the original words 'Doctor' and 'Mister' have remained. Similarly 'Mrs' is a contraction of 'Mistress'. In this case, the first and last letters are used, together with one from the middle.

Another form of abbreviation is the **acronym**. This is a word created by taking the first letter of each word in a phrase. For example, 'NATO' stands for the **N**orth **A**tlantic **T**reaty **O**rganisation. Acronyms are sometimes pronounced as complete words, like NATO. Alternatively, the letters may be spelled out, like V—I—P, which stands for **V**ery **I**mportant **P**erson.

Full stops are usually omitted in abbreviations formed from the initial letters of a phrase like BBC, which stands for the British Broadcasting Corporation, or TUC, the Trades Union Congress.

It is normal to put a full stop after contractions, especially when the shortened form leaves out the last letter of the complete word, like 'co.' for 'company', or 'p.m.', which is short for the Latin phrase '*post meridiem*', meaning 'after noon'.

Activity

Look at this list of shortened words. The date beside them shows the time when they first began to be used. Which words do you think they are shortened forms of? The meaning of the words should give you a clue.

glad 1923	admin 1942	limo 1968	mike 1970
glam 1936	mini 1961	lib 1970	

Where do you come from?

You have already seen how the English language has been expanded as a result of invasions, inventions, accidents, mistakes and the development of the mass media. One of the strongest influences on the way you use language, especially the way you talk, is the area where you grew up. The way you pronounce words is called your **accent**. Everyone has their own accent. There are a number of well-known regional accents and many less well known ones.

Activity

Where do these people come from? What accent do you associate with them?

How many English accents do you know? What are the accents in your area?

The Queen.

Bill Clinton.

Paul Gascoigne.

Kylie Minogue.

Billy Connolly.

Frank Bruno.

Were there any people it was difficult to place? Why?

Investigate

a Find out what accent most of the characters in these soap operas use: *Brookside, EastEnders, Emmerdale Farm, Coronation Street, Neighbours.*

b What accents do the singers in your favourite pop groups have?

c What is your favourite accent? Why?

Accent or dialect?

Most people who speak in a regional **accent** also have a regional **dialect**. However, it is a mistake to think that dialect and accent are the same thing. In fact, speakers of the same dialect may have different accents.

Dialects have at least three main features:

1 They are often spoken with a recognisable accent, for example Geordie.
2 They have special rules about the way sentences and groups of words are put together, for example 'She done it' rather than 'She did it'.
3 They use some items of vocabulary (words) which other dialects do not have, for example 'wee bairn' instead of 'small child'.

In the next two pages you will see how dialects have developed so that some have become more important than others.

This photograph shows a scene from *Pygmalion* by George Bernard Shaw. The play centres around a claim made by Henry Higgins (centre), a professor of phonetics, to his friend Colonel Pickering, that he can pass off a cockney flower-seller, Eliza Doolittle, as a duchess by teaching her to speak without her cockney accent.

HIGGINS I can place any man within six miles. I can place him within two miles in London, sometimes within two streets.

Investigate

No two people use language in exactly the same way. Everyone has their own **idiolect**, the special way in which they use language.

Make a list of the special words used by your friends. Ask your friends to tell you what they think your special ways of using language are.

'Yammerin', bargin' a bucketful and ah diven't knaah

There was a time when different regional accents were hardly ever heard on television. When it first began broadcasting, the BBC deliberately taught its announcers, newsreaders and interviewers to speak with an accent which the first Director General of the BBC hoped 'would not be laughed at in any part of the country'.

A BBC newsreader.

This attempt to produce a 'neutral' way of speaking was not entirely successful. Many people felt it was heavily biased in favour of the polite middle-class speech of the South and South-East of England.

Nowadays many local and national programmes feature speakers who have distinctive local accents. It is less common, however, to find examples of presenters speaking in dialect, using the particular words and phrases that belong exclusively to one area of the country.

Activity

Read these reviews of television programmes. They were written in dialect by young people.

So say the lads an' lasses

Whether they make you yammer or haffle or leave you bargin' a bucketful, you'll be git impressed by these reviews in dialect.

LAST term, *eQ* offered school students the opportunity to become television reviewers. Readers were invited to submit short reviews of a programme of their choice. There was one catch: you had to write the article in the dialect of your area.

More than 300 of you wrote in from all parts of England, Scotland, Wales and Northern Ireland. Some of you interpreted "dialect" as Standard English spelled in a somewhat unconventional manner; a few of you based your reviews on some terms of abuse it would have been difficult to print in a newspaper. Many of you, however, conducted effective research into the idiom, vocabulary and grammar of your local dialect and used it to write lively, opinionated articles. We would have needed scores of pages to print all the interesting reviews we received but the following were chosen as representing some of the best.

HAD yer gobs, lads an' lasses, an' gis a chance to tell yer aboot this git good programme, Spender, every Tuesday neet.

The gen is that this Geordie, Spender, is a copper doon in London right, when his partner (the gadgy he walks with) gets shot. To save his face, Spender is relocated back to his native Tyneside — Geordieland to the rest of us man.

He is met with trouble one moment he arrives, not from any suspects as yer might suss. More from his ex-missus, Frances, two bairns and a bloke called Stick. Stick is Spender's worst nightmare — yer knaah the type, always dodging the fuzz, mixing with the wrang people. But even wor Jimmy Nail (Spender) winnit admit that he actually likes the bloke.

I git really like this programme; it's dead chos, the characters are so real yer feel yer knaah them like they was yer next door neighbours' kids or summit.

Unfortunately the series has finished — ah diven't knaah why, like. I hope with sincerity that the sackless BBC gives iz another chance to observe the Geordie scenario.

Gan carry an' watch it, you'll be git impressed.

Glossary

had yer gobs ...... shut your mouth
gis ...... give me
git ...... very
neet ...... night
gen ...... story/gossip
walks ...... works
Geordieland ...... Newcastle
suss ...... expect
ex-missus ...... ex-wife
bairns ...... children
wrang ...... wrong
bloke ...... man
dead ...... very
chos ...... great
ah diven't knaah ...... I don't know
sackless ...... term used to convey stupidity

DID you see Home and Away this week? There was a whole hanlin' about that wee Sophie one. She cossed a lot a boller. She couldn't read a sign put up by Adam and got electrocuted.

Oul Adam was a trick above his capers when he tried to fix up a cupboard at the surf club. He totally wrecked the place.

Of course, when Pippa found out she was jumpin'. She came in bargin' a bucketful at Adam. Steven was the only other person who knew about Sophie, but he was too bird-mouthed to speak. I couldn't get over Ben becoming engaged to that Carly skitter. To think she went on a diet, imagine her that's so thin she would be reported missing if she stood sideways.

Poor wee Lance has had a face so long the barber would charge him twice to cut his hair since Martin has left.

The wee lad Mullet is as big a liar as John Green but it was a great laugh when he swiped Alf's crab. That Sally can be a right huffy snotter if anything goes wrong.

I thought the show was great but I am very disappointed about that oul rip Celia leaving to go to Africa.

Glossary

hanlin' ...... a tricky situation
cossed ...... caused
boller ...... trouble or aggravation
a trick above his capers ...... pushing his luck
jumpin' ...... very angry, upset
bargin' a bucketful ...... expressing grave displeasure
bird-mouthed ...... reluctant to speak up
skitter ...... dislikeable person
had a face so long the barber would charge him twice to cut his hair ...... down in the dumps
as big a liar as John Green ...... description of a fibber
huffy snotter ...... someone prone to sulking
oul rip ...... gossiping woman

Activity

Which different features of dialect listed on page 49 did you notice in the reviews? What would the Standard English be for these features? How do they differ?

Produce a review of a television programme of your choice. Write it in the dialect of the area where you live or in the dialect used by characters in the programme you are reviewing.

Shamed into talking 'proper'

Prince of Wales says English is taught 'bloody badly'

The Prince of Wales said yesterday that English was taught 'so bloody badly' that even his own office staff could not speak or write the language properly.

The Prince said: 'All the people in my office can't speak properly, can't write properly and can't punctuate. I have to correct all the letters myself. English is taught so bloody badly.'

'I do not believe English is being taught properly. You cannot educate people properly unless you do it on a basic framework and drilling system.'

The Prince, educated at Gordonstoun, Geelong Grammar School, Australia, and Trinity College, Cambridge (where he read History), gave his views on the country's schools – and his staff of 20 – to a group of senior businessmen and chief education officers at the launch in London of the Foundation for Education Business Partnerships, which is aimed at developing closer links between schools and industry.

The Prince, who gained two A levels – a B in history and a C in French – said: 'It is a fundamental problem. We have got to produce people who can write proper English if we want to produce people who can write good plays and good literature for the future. It cannot be done by the present system ... and the nonsense academics come up with.'

The Prince received some support from Mr Kenneth Baker, Secretary of State for Education and Science, who said: 'Prince Charles echoes the concerns of many parents. That is why we are introducing a national curriculum with English as a core subject.

'We have already set out standards for seven year olds which focus on reading, writing, speaking, grammar, spelling and punctuation. High standards have to start in primary schools.'

Mr Baker has fought a running battle with educationists on the teaching of English grammar.

Last week the National Curriculum Council published English guidelines for five to 16-year-olds which do not recommend a return to traditional grammar teaching. The working party, chaired by Professor Brian Cox of Manchester University, agreed that all children should have a knowledge of grammar and know how to speak and write standard English, although phrases such as 'we was' were acceptable at home and between friends.

Mr Doug McAvoy, deputy general secretary of the National Union of Teachers, the largest teachers' union, said: 'Prince Charles should stick to the things he knows about from first hand. It certainly is not teaching and he has not received the benefits of a state education.

'To motivate children, you have to make lessons exciting and interesting, and you do not do that by teaching grammar by rote.'

Mr Nigel de Gruchy, deputy general secretary of the National Association of Schoolmasters and Union of Women Teachers, said: 'I did not realize the Royal Prerogative meant you could ignore all the evidence. More children pass more examinations than ever before. He probably does not pay enough to attract the right quality of people to type his letters.'

Mr de Gruchy added: 'If he has to swear, he is proving that the public schools are as bad as the state ones. It is a case of the pot calling the kettle black.'

Mr Walter Levers, President of the National Association of Headteachers, said: 'The fact is that the vast majority of schools are doing a very good job. There is no evidence that in the past years people could write and spell correctly to a greater extent than they do at the moment.'

'Good English', 'the Queen's English' and 'writing properly' are expressions you may have come across. English is two of the three 'Rs', Reading, Writing and Arithmetic, and everyone wants to be good at them. Many employers agree with Prince Charles and feel that being able to speak and write English well is very important.

The development of Standard English

Key points

- Anyone, wherever they live, can speak Standard English.
- You can speak Standard English with an accent.
- Standard English is one of a number of English dialects.
- It is widely accepted that it is important to be able to use and understand Standard English.

When Caxton and other printers made decisions about spelling, they started the process of standardising written English. Certain ways of spelling words began to be accepted as normal or 'correct'. This process was later continued by Dr Johnson and other compilers of dictionaries and grammar books.

The term **Standard English** refers to the English that is used and understood by speakers and writers of English all over the world. People sometimes think it means 'talking posh', but it can be spoken with a variety of accents.

Some confusion is due to the development of something called **Received Pronunciation** or '**RP**'. RP has its roots in the public schools which blossomed at the end of the nineteenth century. The growth of these schools and the accent that they taught spread throughout the world, as former pupils joined the British Civil Service and went out to work in different parts of the British Empire. This way of speaking naturally became associated with a particular social class, those people who had money and power. It became known as 'the best kind of English ... spoken by those often very properly called the best people'.

RP was the accent adopted by the BBC when it first began broadcasting and some people began to refer to it as 'BBC English'.

It is important to realise that both RP and 'BBC English' are descriptions of accents. Standard English is a dialect – a very special dialect, because it is used world-wide. Any words or phrases which are particular to a local dialect and would not be understood outside that part of the country cannot be described as Standard English.

However, Standard English is always changing. A word which today seems like slang or an example of local dialect may in the future become absorbed into the larger dialect of Standard English. For example, at one time the word 'lunch' was regarded as dreadful slang, but now it is perfectly acceptable.

Activity

What do you think of Standard English? Have you ever been criticised for not speaking properly? Which words were you using?

Have you ever made fun of a new teacher or pupil at your school just because they speak with a different accent? Have you ever made fun of someone for 'talking posh'? Do you judge people by the way they speak? Explain your answers.

A question of register

People speak and behave differently depending on where they are and who they are with. For example, you would introduce yourself in different ways to your best friend, to a very young child, or to your headteacher. This aspect of language is known as **register**. The word 'register' is used to describe the variety of different ways in which we talk.

In deciding how to speak, you make quick decisions about the importance of the person you are addressing, their position and how well you know them. The person or people you are talking to are known as your **audience**. In a typical day you will speak to many different types of audience, and you will often be making decisions about your language unconsciously.

Activity

In groups, read the following short playscripts aloud.

1

JOANNE Did you see that film on the box last night?

STEPHANIE The one about the bloke who kept seeing his old man's ghost?

JOANNE Yeah. What did you think of it?

STEPHANIE Rubbish.

JOANNE That's what I thought. I mean, nothing really happened, did it?

STEPHANIE Talk about boring.

EMMA I thought it was brilliant.

JOANNE You never?

STEPHANIE She's just trying to be clever.

EMMA That's not hard around here.

JOANNE Cheek!

STEPHANIE Look out, here comes Mannering. She don't look very happy.

JOANNE Well I ain't done nothing to annoy her.

STEPHANIE You hope.

(Enter MS MANNERING**.)**

MS MANNERING Joanne, can I have a word with you?

JOANNE Of course. Can I ask what it's in connection with?

MS MANNERING We can talk about that in my office.

JOANNE Do you mind if I just finish this order form first?

MS MANNERING You can do that afterwards. Stephanie, have you copied those letters?

STEPHANIE I beg your pardon?

MS MANNERING Have you done those letters I gave you?

STEPHANIE I'm afraid I forgot them.

MS MANNERING You and Emma had better do them now. They absolutely must go out this morning.

STEPHANIE Right.

2

DONALD What's up with this telly? Has our Billy been messing about with it again?

ELAINE Don't panic. It's just on the video channel, that's all. Here, let me do it.

NEWSREADER Police are looking for an armed man who raided a sub post office in Painton Road yesterday.

(Enter BILLY.**)**

DONALD Have you been fiddling with this telly?

ELAINE Ssh! Listen.

NEWSREADER He was wearing a balaclava helmet and carrying a sawn-off shotgun. The police have appealed for witnesses to come forward. Any information will be treated in the strictest confidence.

ELAINE Did you hear that?

BILLY Hear what?

ELAINE The police are looking for some fella with a shooter who held up a post office.

DONALD So what?

ELAINE I'll tell you 'so what'. I was up in our Billy's bedroom last night.

BILLY What the hell were you doing there?

DONALD You wanna watch your mouth, son.

BILLY That's my room. You've got no business going in there.

ELAINE Oh haven't I? We'll see about that. You sit down mister high and mighty. It's time we had a family conference.

3

JIM What about that new take-away in the High Street?

DAVE You must be joking!

JIM I thought it looked all right.

DAVE Leave it out! I'm not going there.

JIM What's wrong with it, then?

DAVE Steve reckons they catch cats and use them instead of chicken.

JIM Do me a favour!

DAVE He knows a bloke that works in the kitchen.

JIM I bet he does!

DAVE What do you mean?

JIM You don't want to believe a word Steve says.

DAVE Why not?

JIM He's round the twist.

DAVE Says who?

JIM It's common knowledge. He can't stop telling porkies to save his life.

4

MRS GRICE What's the matter, Andrew?

ANDREW Gayle says I can't do Geography and History.

MRS GRICE Why not?

ANDREW I dunno. He just said I can't.

MRS GRICE Which one is he?

ANDREW That's him over there.

MRS GRICE The one sitting by the window?

ANDREW Yeah.

MRS GRICE Mr Gayle. I'm Mrs Grice, Andrew's mother.

MR GAYLE How do you do.

MRS GRICE There seems to be a problem with Andrew's options.

MR GAYLE Yes, well, I did explain to him that two humanities is not really possible.

MRS GRICE But I'm afraid that two humanities is exactly what he wants to do, isn't it Andrew?

ANDREW Yes.

Activity

Read each dialogue through again carefully. In groups, decide which speakers are using Standard English. Do these speakers use *only* Standard English? Which speakers change the way they speak during the dialogue? What causes them to change?

For each speaker, make a list of the things you think might be going through their mind about the person they are talking to.

How many different people do you speak to in a typical day? Make a list of them. Choose three different people. Imagine the different styles of conversation you might have with them. Write it out as a script. (You can see how to set one out from the examples on the previous pages. Remember that you do not need to use speech marks.) Make sure you change your register according to which person is speaking and whom he or she is speaking to.

English as a world language

The top ten languages

	Mother-tongue speakers	
1	Chinese – Mandarin	1,000 million
2	English	350 million
3	Spanish	250 million
4	Hindi	200 million
5	Arabic	150 million
6	Bengali	150 million
7	Russian	150 million
8	Portuguese	135 million
9	Japanese	120 million
10	German	100 million

Apart from Mandarin, which is spoken by one thousand million people, mostly living in China, English is the most widely used language in the world. It is certainly the language spoken in more countries than any other.

Activity

Which European languages did you expect to appear in the top ten?

Why do Spanish, Portuguese and English appear, but not French?

The European Parliament.

Investigate

Find out which countries use English as their official language. Draw or trace a world map and mark the English-speaking countries on it.

Activity

Why do you think that English is so widely spoken and understood throughout the world? Make a list of all the ways in which it is possible to encounter English in countries outside Britain.

Investigate

Find out:

a what proportion of English speakers live in Britain

b which other languages are spoken in Britain and in your school.

Making assumptions about language

Read this story carefully.

In the hands of the expert

The lights ahead were red. The driver bit his lip and pushed his foot down hard on the accelerator. He couldn't afford to waste a second. With its blue light flashing and its siren wailing, the ambulance shot through the busy road junction.

In the back, the paramedic looked anxiously at his patient. Care was about the only thing he could give him right now. What he needed was a skilled surgeon, but the paramedic wasn't sure they would find the right one up ahead.

Schedules, rotas, shifts – that was what the hospital administration would have to take into consideration. Who was on duty this evening? Was there sufficient free space in the emergency department? Did they have the beds? Did they have the right surgeon?

The paramedic's gaze rested on the blood-stained blankets. He wasn't a doctor, of course. He'd only been a paramedic for six months. Before that, for years, he was just a plain, ordinary ambulance driver's mate. But he knew a thing or two. And he knew there was only one surgeon who could bring this boy back from certain death. If that surgeon wasn't on duty tonight, there was no hope at all.

The paramedic put out a hand to grab the restraining strap as the ambulance driver went round a corner without changing gear. He didn't need to look out the window to know exactly where they were. Ward's Corner, it was called, after the big department store that had taken up one whole block when he was a boy. There was no more Ward's now, of course. The supermarkets and the precinct had proved too much competition. But the corner still kept its name. A lot of things had changed since those days. The traffic on the road, for example. He could remember playing football in a street near here when he was a boy. Not much chance of that now.

After Ward's Corner they were nearly there. The paramedic knew the ambulance would screech through the hospital gates in exactly six minutes, assuming there weren't any snags.

No, the snags were all on the other side of the hospital gates. Would this young boy get the surgeon he needed? Or was he destined to become another unfortunate hospital statistic? Even ten and a half years as an ambulance driver's mate and six months as a paramedic didn't harden you to the carnage you saw regularly in road accidents. Tonight's was worse than usual. The fact that the victims were father and son somehow made it even worse.

He looked at the other bed, next to the boy's, the one with the blanket pulled up over the man's face. Not even the greatest surgeon in the world could do anything about him. He had been in the driver's seat. He had died instantly. Probably hadn't known a thing about it – just one moment of searing pain and then, goodnight.

The paramedic shuddered. It was a hard world and it got harder every day. He hoped he would die in his sleep. He wondered about the rest of the family. Some poor so-and-so would have to break the news to them. The local beat constable, probably. 'Excuse me, madam. I'm afraid I have some bad news for you.' Well, at least that wasn't his job.

The ambulance passed through the hospital gates and pulled up outside the accident and emergency department. The paramedic opened the back doors as the ambulance driver came round to help him lift down the stretchers.

'Not that one,' he said, as the driver reached for the dead man's stretcher. 'He's had it. It's the son we've got to get down first.'

The driver nodded. He wasn't the talkative type.

The emergency team was waiting as they came through the swing doors. 'Okay, we'll take him from here,' a young nurse said. She smiled at the paramedic.

'Is there another patient?' the sister asked.

'Father and son,' the paramedic replied. 'But there's nothing you can do for him.'

The stretcher was already being rushed away down the corridor, with blood transfusion apparatus strapped on. He turned to go back to the ambulance for the second time.

'Who is on duty tonight?' he said, over his shoulder.

'Just bring the patient,' the sister ordered briskly. 'Leave the rest to us.'

He nodded. 'Don't say thank you,' he muttered to himself.

In the operating theatre, the team went efficiently through their routine. They knew what needed to be done. There was little conversation between them. They were waiting now for the one person who could make a difference.

At last the surgeon walked in. The team looked up for a moment and felt their confidence grow. Everyone knew that this surgeon could earn a fortune in private practice. What made someone with such skill stay in an underpaid, stressful life? They knew the answer to that as well: dedication and the desire to bring help where it was most needed.

The anaesthetist, nurses and junior doctor who were gathered round the operating table felt they were privileged to be part of this team. They were being led by a real expert.

The surgeon nodded to them all in turn, then walked over to the boy on the stretcher and stopped.

The team waited. Not a word was spoken. The only sound was the bleeping of the machine which was measuring the patient's fragile heartbeat. All the colour seemed to have drained from the surgeon's face.

The junior doctor looked up questioningly. 'Is there something wrong?' he asked. The team-leader, the expert, the one they all looked up to, seemed to be trembling.

'What is it?' the junior doctor said. 'What's the matter?'

'My son!' the surgeon said.

The others looked round in amazement.

How could this be?

Activity

How could this be (see page 62)? The answer is obvious, and you have probably heard versions of stories like this one. Many people still take a moment to work it out.

Language and work

Activity

Imagine you are a magazine journalist. You have to think up false names to conceal the identities of a group of people you have just interviewed. Below is a list of the occupations of your interviewees:

1 Managing Director of a large company
2 Secretary
3 Hairdresser
4 Headteacher of a large school
5 Doctor in a busy practice
6 Electrician
7 Car mechanic
8 Glamorous model

Think of a first and last name for each of these characters. When you have finished, turn to the bottom of page 63.

Activity

How many job titles can you think of which have the word 'man' in them? Brainstorm all you can think of and see how many you have. What others ways are there of showing gender in a job title?

Investigate

How many alternative names can you think of for the job titles given here? For example, 'politician' for 'statesman' or 'fire-fighter' for 'fireman'. Do you think it matters that job titles assume a certain gender?

Fireman
Postman
Statesman

Activity

What do you think is odd about the way the five people have been listed on this notice?

C. Benn
R. S. Churchill
Carolyn Jenkins (Mrs Jenkins)
J. Lemmon
Judith Trim (Miss)

Dr Mr Mrs
Ms Rev'd Miss

You have already seen how easy it is to make assumptions about people's gender and how our choice of language shows this. There is also a heavy bias towards men in the way we use titles. For example, there are three different ways of describing women: Miss, Mrs and Ms whereas there is only one, Mr, which is normally used for men. This means that if you are a woman, people are given more information about your personal life.

Answer to *In the hands of the expert*
The surgeon is the boy's mother.

Language can be sexist

Not surprisingly, many women take offence at the way in which language implies that they are less important or less capable than men.

One of the main stumbling blocks comes in using the word 'he'. If you are clearly describing a man, then there is no problem. If, on the other hand, you are talking about people in general – men and women – then you are using language which assumes that everyone *is*, in fact, male. This is an example of **sexist language**.

In the USA, women have made a lot of this issue. As a direct result of women making people more aware of such sexism, the use of 'he' and 'man', where 'he/she' and 'people' are implied, has decreased. Between 1971 and 1979, a survey of magazines and newspapers was carried out. It found that in 1971, 12.3 words in every 5,000 were sexist. By 1979, the figure had dropped to 4.3 words in every 5,000 words. Many papers now say 's/he' and 'he or she'.

man in the street

Dear Sir

man to man

thinking man

Joe public

history of mankind

statesman

masterplan

masterpiece

mastermind

Here we are at home, says Daddy.

Peter helps Daddy with the car, and Jane helps Mummy get the tea.

Good girl, says Mummy to Jane.

You are a good girl to help me like this.

Good good girl

Investigate

How many of the textbooks and novels which you read contain examples of what you consider to be sexist language? Make a survey of them as a class and present your findings as a wall-chart.

Language and work: activity

Did you choose male names for 1, 4, 5, 6 and 7 and female for 2 and 8 with either for 3? How many of your fellow students did the same? Was there any difference between the boys and the girls on this matter?

three LOOK WHO'S TALKING

Starting point

Simone and Kathleen are two eleven-year-old girls. Simone is staying the night with Kathleen. They are going to watch a video from a sofa bed. First they have to make the bed.

KATHLEEN	Right, so we need to put the sheet on first.
SIMONE	Kathleen?
KATHLEEN	Yeah.
SIMONE	(*Lies down on the bed*) This is my bed. (*Laughs*) This is my bed.
KATHLEEN	(*Laughing*) Get the sheet.
SIMONE	(*Giggling*) I'll just lie on here for a while. It's lovely. Just lie on here. It's lovely.
KATHLEEN	No, let me get it.
SIMONE	I'll stay here. I think I'll just stay here, I think. Oh, this is lovely.
KATHLEEN	No. Get the sheet. Get the sheet. Get the sheet.
SIMONE	Oh Kathleen. This is my bed.
KATHLEEN	No. Help me put the sheet on, please.
SIMONE	I may actually. I may not. I don't...
KATHLEEN	(*Interrupts*) I don't...
KATHLEEN	I don't like sleeping on there. } (*Together*)
SIMONE	But I can't.
SIMONE	Huh?
KATHLEEN	I don't like sleeping on there.
SIMONE	Isn't it nice?
KATHLEEN	It's all right.

SIMONE You can't really see the TV, can you?

KATHLEEN No.

SIMONE Then even if I am sleeping there I have to get up again to uh… see… if I'm… if I can watch telly there, yeah?

KATHLEEN Yeah?

SIMONE No. If I uh… I watch telly there?

KATHLEEN Yeah.

SIMONE And if I am sleeping there, I have to get out and go over there.

KATHLEEN Yeah, I know. And it will be cold.

SIMONE Go on.

SIMONE Have we done my side? } (*Together*)

KATHLEEN Cold.

KATHLEEN It will be cold. You have to tuck it under.

SIMONE I have. Help me do my side. I like mine puffy.

KATHLEEN Don't make it too… Ow!

SIMONE What happened?

KATHLEEN You're making all your side puffy.

SIMONE All right, I'll just leave it. Okay?

KATHLEEN Right.

SIMONE Right, that's about equal.

Private conversation has a number of typical features.

It contains:

- repeated words
- 'ums' and 'ers' and 'huhs'
- words which do not appear to follow on from what has just been said
- words, especially nouns, on their own without verbs.
- different versions of words, like 'yeah' for 'yes'

Investigate

Tape-record yourself or members of your family while you are carrying out a simple task. Play the tape back and note down examples of the features listed above. Can you think of any other typical examples of spoken English?

Patterns of speech

Spoken English is very different from English that is only written down. It is often not until you see a **transcript**, an exact written version of speech, 'ers' and 'ums' included, that you fully realise this.

Look at the illustration below. Much of what you say is part of a standard pattern of words used for particular situations. You are probably not even aware that you are doing this.

These kinds of expression are often used when people meet each other or say goodbye. They are all versions of the same basic 'hello' or 'goodbye' idea. They do not really have much meaning in themselves, but help to get a conversation going.

Activity

How many ways can you think of for saying 'hello' or 'goodbye'? Which do you use most often?

How many ways can you think of for apologising and responding to an apology? In pairs, role-play a number of situations in which this kind of exchange of language takes place. Act them out to the rest of the class. Build up a class list of the many different patterns of speech used in apologising.

Investigate

What other expressions can you think of which are similar to the examples given? Think, for instance, of situations where people are congratulating each other, making someone feel at ease or excusing themselves for some reason.

Speeding up

Do you always speak at the same speed? Has anyone ever asked you to speak more slowly? The answer to the second question is probably 'yes', because we all change the speed we talk at according to the situation we are in.

Activity

In pairs, one of you gives the other a piece of bad news, or passes on something that they know will offend the other person. If you try to do this as realistically as possible, you will notice that some parts of your conversation are faster than others. This is because we tend to speed up if what we are saying is embarrassing or difficult. Can you think of any other examples of situations in which you speak faster?

Investigate

Tape-record or listen to a group of your friends talking together. When do people speed up? What do you think the reasons are for this?

Being economical with words

When you are speaking, it is often possible to communicate ideas with very few words, especially when the setting of the conversation is known. This is much harder to do when you are writing.

Activity

In groups, work out what you think these words mean and what is happening. For each of these groups of words, imagine and then act out the rest of the conversation.

The origins of language

How did language start? Where did it start? Have there always been so many different languages in the world? People have been asking these and other similar questions for many centuries.

There are a number of theories about how language began. Some think that people began to copy the sounds of animals, others think that words came from the instinctive sound people made when they felt pain, anger or other strong emotions.

The truth is that no one really knows. It is possible to work out from very old skulls that, at a certain time in the development of human beings, there came a moment when we had sufficiently advanced vocal chords to be able to speak.

But we can only guess about what kind of language came out of the mouths of early people. We can also only guess as to which language started where, and therefore how the languages from which English grew emerged.

Read this famous story of the Tower of Babel, which has been adapted from the first book in the Bible, Genesis.

The Tower of Babel

In the early days of the world there was just one language. There weren't very many words in it, but that didn't matter because few words were needed at that time. People understood each other easily, much more easily than they do now, even though we now have many more words.

At first people wandered about the earth, migrating from one place to another. But then they came to the land of Shinar and they decided to settle there. They learnt how to make bricks from clay and how to use bitumen as mortar. They learnt how to make buildings with these bricks, and they became very proud of what they had achieved.

Then a new idea began to take shape among them. No one was sure who had the idea first, but they all agreed that it was a wonderful idea. They would build a tower and it would be so high that it would reach Heaven itself. The top of the tower would disappear into the clouds. It would stand out on the plain, like a finger pointing towards the sky.

Now God looked down from Heaven and saw the people toiling on the plain to build the tower. He shook his head in dismay. 'This is just the beginning,' he said to himself. 'Soon there will be no stopping these people. They are united, they all speak the same language and nothing which they decide to do will be impossible for them. I must put a stop to this.'

So God decided that he would go down to the Earth, to the plain of Shinar and confuse their language. And that is what he did. Suddenly the workers on the tower found that they could not understand each other. They looked around them in amazement, for instead of words that had meaning, each person heard the others speaking in strange sounds, sometimes harsh, sometimes musical, but always without any meaning to the listener.

For some time they carried on trying to communicate, making signs and babbling at each other in a dozen different languages. But at last they saw that it was useless. One by one they put down their tools and went back to their homes in despair.

The next morning they woke, hoping to find that it had all been no more than an unpleasant dream. Eagerly they sprang from their beds and went outside their houses to greet each other. But their faces fell. For each man greeted his fellow with an unfamiliar word and every woman spoke to her neighbour in an unknown tongue. They knew then that it had not been a dream and that there was no escaping the truth. Many of them stood outside their houses and wept.

Wearily they made their way back to the tower and tried to begin again the job on which they had all been working together. But they had lost heart and soon the plain of Shinar, which had echoed to the sound of tools working on stone, was silent.

In time they began to wander away from the plain of Shinar, for there was no point in living together when no one could understand anyone else. The tower still stood half-finished, and so it remained. Those who came afterwards called it the Tower of Babel.

The people of Shinar scattered abroad across the whole of the Earth, and wherever they went they took their new languages with them. And that is why the peoples of the Earth all speak in different languages now, though once they all knew a common tongue.

(Adapted from Genesis 2: 1–10.)

Activity

How do you think language began? How do you think different languages might have developed?

Write your own story in which you describe how language began.

Investigate

What are the first words that people generally learn in a new language? Look at the textbooks you use in your French or German lessons to help you. Make a list of the most common words or expressions you find.

Do you think this would have been the same for early people living in caves or simple shelters? What words do you think might have been most important for them? Compare your two lists. What are the differences between them? How could you explain these differences?

Language and identity

You have already seen how everyone has a particular dialect and a particular accent. But there are also other more personal things about the way you use language which make you very much an individual person.

Activity

Perhaps the most important piece of personal language you have is your first name. Look at this list of the most popular names for new-born babies in England in 1988:

Girls	Boys
1 Rebecca	1 Daniel
2 Sarah	2 Christopher
3 Emma	3 Michael
4 Laura	4 James
5 Rachel	5 Matthew
6 Samantha	6 Andrew
7 Charlotte	7 Adam
8 Kirsty	8 Thomas
9 Nicola	9 David
10 Amy	10 Richard

Why do you think parents choose a particular name for their baby? Which of these names do you like most? Is your name in the 'top ten'? Do you like your own name?

It is an obvious but important fact that we do not choose our own names. Some people like their name, others do not. Long names are often shortened, and even short ones are made shorter. For example, 'Rebecca' becomes 'Becky' and 'Daniel' becomes 'Dan'. How many short forms of the names in the list above can you think of?

Activity

Carry out a survey of names of pupils in your year. Which are the ten most popular names for girls and boys?

Private languages

You are marked out as an individual not only by your name, but also by the way you use language. It is likely that no two people speak English in exactly the same way – everyone is different. An individual's distinctive way of speaking is called their **idiolect**.

Activity

How conscious are you of the particular way you use language? In groups, ask your friends whether:

a you use any special words not used by others
b pronounce any words in a particular way
c you speak differently when you are with different people at school
d you speak differently from your parents.

Get them to make a list of the special ways in which you use English.

Investigate

Most families have certain words, 'family' words, which are private to them. Some families even have private languages.

Make a list of all the special words or expressions you use at home and compare it with others in your class.

The case of Timothy Evans

In 1950 Timothy Evans was hanged for the murder of his wife and child. An important piece of evidence in the case was a confession he apparently made to the police. Evans could hardly read or write, so his statement was written down for him.

At the trial he denied his confession, but he was nevertheless sentenced to death. Sixteen years after his death Evans was pardoned when the language used in his statement was looked at in detail. It was decided that two very different styles of language were used, so Evans's statement must have been partly made up by someone else!

Read these two extracts from Evans's statement:

'**I done my day's work** and then had an argument with the **Guvnor** then I left the job. **He give me** my wages before I went home.'

'She was **incurring one debt after another** and I could not stand it any longer so I strangled her with a piece of rope and took her down to the flat below the same night **whilst** the old man was in hospital.'

Activity

Look closely at the phrases in bold type in the two extracts. Why are they significant?

What's in a word?

BOYCOTT CHAUVINIST MESMERISE

We aren't usually aware of the history of the words we use. For example, we talk of 'boycotting' something or 'hoovering' the carpet, without realising that Boycott and Hoover were real people. Words like these which are formed using someone's name are called **eponyms**. In some cases the people behind the words would be horrified to hear how their names are now being used.

HOOVER

BIRO

Read how these two characters became immortalised in the English language.

Boycott

Charles Cunningham Boycott was a British cavalry officer in the mid-nineteenth century. He was known as a stiff, rather difficult man. At that time, the whole of Ireland was ruled by Britain. Many landlords who rented out their property in Ireland lived in England and employed agents to run their Irish estates. After leaving his regiment, Boycott got a job as the agent on an estate in County Mayo.

The conditions which tenants endured were terribly hard. If they could not pay their rent, they were thrown out of their homes. Many agents were worse than Boycott, but he had a knack of annoying people. For example, he infuriated the locals by fining them whenever their hens trespassed on his land.

Finally, the local community banded together. Everyone refused to work on Boycott's fields, and the blacksmith would not shoe his horse. His servants walked out. Boycott tried harvesting his own crops, but no one would buy them. In the end, he returned to England financially ruined.

Mesmer

Friedrich Anton Mesmer was an eighteenth-century doctor who developed a theory of animal magnetism. He claimed that it was a force present in all of us, and he used it to 'cure' patients, especially those with nervous disorders. Mesmer had some spectacular successes in treating people, but his methods were eventually rejected.

People continued to be influenced by his theories and, in 1843, Dr James Braid, a Scottish surgeon, described the state into which Mesmer put his patients as one of 'hypnosis'.

Since Mesmer's time, we have used the word 'mesmerising' to describe something which really fascinates us or holds our attention. Similarly, when someone seems spellbound by something, we might describe him or her as being 'mesmerised'.

Activity

All of the words at the top of this page are eponyms. Look at the list of eponyms below: Do you use any of them in your everyday speech? Can you think of any others?

MACKINTOSH TARMAC LEVIS MG SELLOTAPE

Slang

Slang is a kind of informal English which is used by a particular group of people, a special language they use when talking together. Gangs often have their special words, as do different groups of workers. Slang is not Standard English and is, therefore, not considered appropriate language in many situations.

One of the most famous kinds is rhyming slang. For example: 'You'll never Adam and Eve it. I've just heard on the dog and bone that Alf's got cash and carried.' Translated, this means: 'You'll never believe it. I've just heard on the telephone that Alf's got married.'

Arthur Daley from *Minder* uses rhyming slang.

Activity

How many examples of rhyming slang do you know? In groups, look at the examples given here, add any expressions which you know, and try to have a conversation in this kind of slang.

bull and a cow	row
Cain and Abel	table
la-di-dah	car
pen and ink	stink
trouble and strife	wife
whistle and flute	suit

eno yob rouf tekram filth nick screw snout

Investigate

There are many other kinds of slang. Can you work out the two groups in the list above?

In many schools different years and different groups have their own slang. Do you? If you do, make a list, like the one for rhyming slang above, to explain what your slang means. Why do you think people use slang?

How many types of slang can you think of?

She really made a fool of herself.

We're just good friends.

It is important to be able to use language in a lively and interesting way. One way of doing this is to use an **idiom**. An idiom is a group of words that does not mean exactly what it seems to. For example, if you've 'lost your voice', you haven't really lost it, you're just unable to speak because you've got a sore throat.

Sometimes idioms or groups of words become so overused that they begin to lose their effect, like 'she was a legend in her own lifetime'. Such phrases are called **clichés**. Sometimes it is difficult to be sure whether you are dealing with an idiom or a cliché.

Read this fictional account of a boxer losing his temper.

Boxer runs amok in night-club

HEAVYWEIGHT BOXER Billy Blake found himself in one fight too many last night when police were called to Charlie's night-club in London's West End.

Blake, thought by many to be over the hill these days, had been drinking with a friend, whose birthday it was. But what started as a small celebration soon got completely out of hand. Apparently Blake went totally overboard and flew off the handle when one of the party suggested that he was past it.

Blake, who is a big man, has a reputation for throwing his weight around, both in and out of the ring. Even though he has gone to seed in the last few years, he is still a force to be reckoned with, and four of the club's bouncers were not enough to control him.

Witnesses said that he ran riot, like a bull in a china shop. Pub customers hid under tables as punches flew all around them. One regular described the scene like this: 'He was sitting there one minute cool as a cucumber, then all of a sudden he went completely round the bend.'

The barman, John Brown, had a similar tale to tell. 'He just went completely bananas. I knew I didn't have a hope in hell of controlling the situation. So I got down behind the bar and waited till the coast was clear. As soon as he was looking the other way I rushed out, made a beeline for the nearest phone-box and called

She gave him a flea in his ear.

I've lost my voice.

Activity

How many idioms do you recognise in this story? How many clichés are there? How many groups of words fall somewhere between being a cliché and being an idiom? In pairs, make three lists, one for idioms, one for clichés, and one for those in between.

In groups, brainstorm as many examples of idioms and clichés as you can think of. How many can you come up with?

Write a newspaper article of your own using a mixture of idioms and clichés.

Investigate

How many idioms can you find in French or German or any other language?

the police.'

Officers arrived at the club in the nick of time. Blake had just seized an ornamental sword from the wall. 'If we hadn't arrived when we did,' said Detective Inspector Keegan, 'there's no telling what he might have done.'

Blake is rumoured to have earned more than a million pounds in his last fight with Louis Capaciono, but friends and associates have pointed out that he spends money like water. Last night's little affair is going to cost him a tidy sum in damages. It might even bring down the curtain on Blake's career altogether if the British Boxing Board of Control rules that Blake's behaviour has brought the sport into disrepute.

Blake's wife, Rita, was keeping tight-lipped as she left the house for work this morning, but friends of the family hint that she is prepared to let her husband stew in his own juice. Perhaps she believes that a few nights behind bars will help him cool off. He certainly needs to keep a low profile for some time, and while he is locked away he is unlikely to get up to any more mischief.

However, it may be too late for Blake to repair the damage. Many people in the business believe that he has definitely gone too far this time. Bert Scuttle, the Board of Control's president, refused to be drawn. 'It's early days yet,' he said. 'We're looking into the matter. We have to wait until we hear both sides of the story. We will reach our decision in good time.' But others were not so optimistic. 'If you ask me,' said Blake's sparring partner, Harry 'Pugnose' Benson, 'poor old Billy's well and truly up the creek this time – without a paddle.'

Saying what you think

From a very early age you use language to express pain and pleasure. If you listen to a baby beginning to talk, he or she will babble away if happy and yell and scream if unhappy. This is a basic but important use of language.

If you are cross or hurt you probably also use language to help you get rid of some of your feelings. Language is a kind of safety valve in this respect.

Sometimes people go one stage further and swear or shout when they are angry. Although people often express concern about the use of 'bad language', swearing or cursing is not a new idea.

Activity

Read aloud these curses and insults taken from Shakespeare's plays. How do they sound? Can you guess what they mean?

Peace good tickle-brain	Goats and monkeys
Sweep on you fat and greasy citizens	You small grey-coated gnat
Pish	Vile worm
You crusty botch of nature	You are a hungry lean-faced villain

Words or thoughts?

For many years, people have wondered which came first, ideas or words. Did the first cave people, for example, think up the word 'fire', or did they point to a pile of wood with the idea in their minds of starting a fire? Like the chicken and the egg, it is not easy to be sure which came first. Clearly words and thoughts are very closely connected, but it is not easy to say which leads to the other.

Activity

Some English words clearly indicate what the person using them thinks of other people.

Look at the two sets of words here. How are they different? What do the words tell you about their user's attitudes?

kids	children
teenagers	young people
posh	well brought up
stuck-up	well-educated

Le Regard intérieur by René Magritte (1898–1967).

Most people wonder why words are as they are, and what would happen if they were all changed. Some writers have even experimented with language in this way (see the extract below).

Activity

Read this extract in which a lonely old man who is fed up with life finds out that, by changing the meanings of words, he can change his world.

So he got up, dressed, sat down on his alarm clock and rested his arms on the table. But the table was no longer called table, it was now called carpet. So in the morning the man left his picture, got dressed, sat down at the carpet on the alarm clock and wondered what to call what.

He called the bed picture.
He called the table carpet.
He called the chair alarm clock.
He called the newspaper bed.
He called the mirror chair.
He called the alarm clock photograph album.
He called the wardrobe newspaper.
He called the carpet wardrobe.
He called the picture table.
And he called the photograph album mirror.

So, in the morning the old man would lie in picture for a long time. At nine the photograph album rang, the man got up and stood on the wardrobe so that his feet wouldn't feel cold, then he took his clothes out of the newspaper, dressed, looked into the chair on the wall, then sat down on the alarm clock at the carpet and turned the pages of his mirror until he found his mother's table.

Activity

See what happens if you change around the meanings of words. Make up a story of your own in which this happens. Or continue the one you have just read.

Inventing a new language

Although English is spoken in many different countries and is currently the main language of international communication, it is only one of hundreds of different languages. Even in Europe many different languages are spoken. If an English person wants to understand a speaker from Italy, she or he will have to either learn Italian or hope that the Italian speaks English.

In an attempt to overcome these difficulties, a man called Dr Zamenhof invented a new language in 1887. He called it **Esperanto**. In the next few pages you will find out more about Esperanto and, in doing so, will see just how irregular English is as a language.

Dr Zamenhof intended Esperanto to be a second language that everyone could learn. At that time, French, rather than English, was the language of international communication. Today there are thousands of people spread over more than one hundred countries who can speak or understand some Esperanto.

Supporters of Esperanto argue that:

- it is the easiest language in the world to learn
- it has been tested for over a hundred years
- learning it will help people to understand more about their own language.

Although there are many enthusiastic Esperanto speakers, it has not yet really caught on as an international language.

Activity

In groups, talk about whether you think an invented international language is a good idea. Can you think of reasons why Esperanto has not caught on?

About Esperanto

Look at this basic fact sheet about Esperanto. If there are any terms you do not understand, ask your English or Languages teacher to explain.

A GLANCE AT ESPERANTO

The Esperanto alphabet has 28 letters: Aa, Bb, Cc Ĉĉ, Dd, Ee, Ff, Gg, Ĝĝ, Hh, Ĥĥ, Ii, Jj, Ĵĵ, Kk, Ll, Mm, Nn, Oo, Pp, Rr, Ss, Ŝŝ, Tt, Uu, Ŭŭ, Vv, Zz. There is no q, w, x or y.

A, E, I, O, U have approximately the vowel sounds heard in *Are theEre thrEE Or twO?*

Diphthongs AJ, EJ, OJ, UJ, AŬ sound as in *whY trAIn bOY drUIds nOW?*

J is like Y in *Yes*
G always sounds as in *Go*
C sounds like TS in *biTS*.

The sounds Ĉ, Ĝ, Ĥ, Ĵ, Ŝ and Ŭ are as heard in *church, George, loch, pleasure, shoe and way*.

No silent letters. Stress always on the last syllable but one.

Absolute regularity—only one way to write any sound, one way to pronounce any spelling.

All grammar is based on a small number of fundamental rules with no exceptions whatsoever.

Parts of speech are formed by adding the appropriate endings to the root words.

O is the ending for all nouns (names of things)

fakto .... *fact*
distanco .... *distance*
libro .... *book*

Adjectives (describing words) end in **A**

granda .... *big*
hela .... *bright*
amuza .... *funny*

to form plurals **J** is added to the end

pezaj libroj — *heavy books*

There are just six endings to all verbs:

infinitive	*present*	*past*	*future*	*conditional*	*imperative*	
I	**AS**	**IS**	**OS**	**US**	**U**	
esti	estas	estis	estos	estus	estu	*to be, etc.*
lerni	lernas	lernis	lernos	lernus	lernu	*to learn, etc.*
legi	legas	legis	legos	legus	legu	*to read, etc.*

N marks the accusative (direct object). Adverbs end in **E**

La libro amuzus vin, se vi legus ĝin atente
The book would amuse you, if you were to read it properly

Numerals 1 to 10: unu, du, tri, kvar, kvin, ses, sep, ok, naŭ, dek
dek tri =13, tridek = 30, sesdek ok = 68, cent = 100
mil = 1000, mil okcent okdek sep = 1887

Activity

Compare English and Esperanto in the following ways.

- How many examples of English words with silent letters can you think of, for example 'knight'?
- All nouns in Esperanto have '-o' at the end of the word. How many different letters appear at the end of nouns in English, for example 'k' in 'book'?
- To make the past tense in Esperanto, you just add '-is' to the end of a verb. How many different ways of making the past tense in English can you think of?
- To make a plural in Esperanto, you add '-j'. How many different kinds of plural in English can you think of?

Could you make up a simple list of rules for English like the ones for Esperanto?

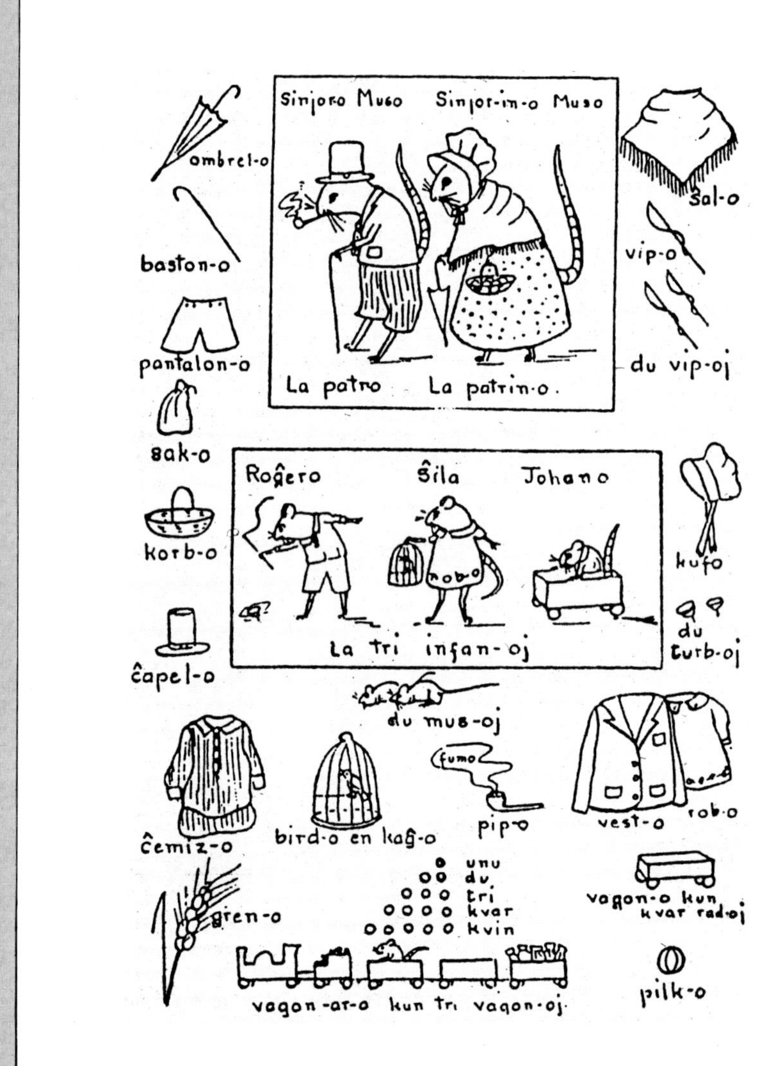

Here are some examples of Esperanto sentences:

La auto estas rapida.

La autobuso estas granda.

Muso estas malgranda.

Rozo estas bela.

A first lesson in Esperanto

Here is a first lesson in Esperanto. It uses a direct method and only uses Esperanto with pictures. How much of it can you understand? Do you think it is a good way of learning a new language?

1

LA FAMILI-O

Est-as kvin person-oj en la famili-o de Sinjor-o Mus-o; patr-o, patr-in-o, kaj tri infan-oj.
Sinjor-o Mus-o est-as la patr-o.
Sinjor-in-o Mus-o est-as la patr-in-o.
Roĝero, Ŝila kaj Johano est-as la tri infan-oj.
Roĝero est-as la fil-o de Sinjor-o kaj Sinjor-in-o Mus-o.
Johano ankaŭ est-as ili-a fil-o.
Ŝila est-as ili-a fil-in-o.
Roĝero est-as la frat-o de Ŝila kaj Johano.
Johano est-as la frat-o de Roĝero kaj Ŝila.
Ŝila est-as la frat-in-o de Roĝero kaj Johano.
Roĝero est-as knab-o. Li port-as pantalon-on kaj ĉemiz-on.
Johano ankaŭ est-as knab-o. Li ankaŭ port-as pantalon-on kaj ĉemiz-on.
Sed Ŝila est-as knab-in-o. Ŝi port-as rob-on.
La patr-o hav-as baston-on kaj pip-on.
Li fum-as la pip-on. Fum-o ven-as el la pip-o.
La patr-in-o hav-as ombrel-on kaj korb-on.
En la korb-o est-as kvin ov-oj.
Roĝero hav-as vip-on. Jes, li hav-as vip-on.
Ŝila ne hav-as vip-on; sed ŝi hav-as bird-on.
Johano ne hav-as vip-on, kaj li ne hav-as bird-on; sed li hav-as vagon-on.

four HAVE YOU HEARD THE ONE ABOUT...?

By word of mouth

Once human beings were able to communicate properly, they began to think of other things to do with words. They soon began to tell each other stories.

Of course, the first stories did not just suddenly appear. They grew, little by little. Each person who heard a story would add their own twists or details, so that the stories changed as they travelled from place to place.

Until it became common to write down stories, the tellers of tales had only their memories to rely on. Their stories had patterns and often contained repeated sections. These tales are called **oral stories**.

Not all the stories were complete. Some were mere fragments, hints and puzzles to tease the listener. Puzzles made of words are called **riddles**. They are generally short, easy to remember and fun. They demand an instant reaction. After all, a riddle is really a story without an ending. The listeners have to provide the ending by solving the puzzle.

Riddles can be about quite simple things or about something as complicated as the meaning of life.

For example, here is an old Egyptian riddle:

> What has four legs in the morning, two legs in the afternoon and three in the evening?

The way to solve this is to think imaginatively. The word 'legs' could be used to mean a number of different things. The answer to this riddle is: a person.

Activity

In groups, see how many of the following riddles you can solve (answers at the bottom of the page):

1 *Two legs sat upon three legs.*
With one leg in his lap.
In comes four legs,
Runs away with one leg,
Two legs picks up three legs,
Throws it after four legs
And makes him bring back one leg.

2 *Without a voice it cries,*
Without a wing it flies,
Without a tooth it bites,
Without a mouth it mutters.

3 *This thing all things devours—*
Birds, beasts, trees and flowers.
Gnaws iron, bites steel,
Grinds hard stones to meal,
Slays kings, ruins town,
And beats high mountains down.

4 *A box with no handle, hinges or lid,*
But golden treasure inside is hid.
What is it?

5 *Under the carpet, up in the air.*
Wherever you look, you'll find me there.
You can't avoid me. I'm like an old friend.
And everyone turns to me in the end.

Some of these riddles involve imaginative thinking. Others are really tricks. Some describe everyday objects as ingeniously as they can. Some riddles were invented to try to explain more complicated ideas which people did not fully understand at the time.

Investigate

Find as many riddles as you can. See if you can decide whether they are just puzzles, or whether they have a deeper meaning.

Answers to riddles

1 'Two legs': a man, 'one leg': leg of mutton, 'four legs': a dog, 'three legs': a stool.
2 The wind.
3 Time.
4 An egg.
5 Dust.

Stories with a message

Some early stories, called **fables**, were similar to riddles, in that the listener was expected to solve them. In this case the listener did not have to find a hidden meaning. Instead, she or he had to uncover the moral of the story. Fables were not just intended for entertainment. They were also meant to make people behave better.

Activity

Fables, like riddles, are found all over the world. Very often they describe animals acting like humans. Read the following fables from Africa and Asia. What do you think the moral is in each case?

The test of friendship (Central Africa)

In the African jungle there is a village where the animals take it in turns to be chief. One year it was the lizard's turn. She dressed for the ceremony but still needed some feathers for her head-dress.

She went to see her best friend, the guinea-fowl. The guinea-fowl had beautiful feathers and the finest of all were on the top of her head. When the lizard asked her for these, the guinea-fowl nearly wept. But the lizard pleaded with her and, in the end, the guinea-fowl plucked the feathers out.

The next year it was the guinea-fowl's turn to be leader. She came to see the lizard. 'There is one thing I need for the ceremony', she said, 'and that is a skin to sit on.'

The lizard had to cut off her skin and hand it over. Without her skin she became very cold and sad and at last she died.

When the other animals heard about this they agreed that it was most unwise to ask a friend for more than she was willing to give. One day she would ask for the favour to be returned.

The tailor-bird and the cat (Bengal)

A tailor-bird had made her nest in a tree that grew in the backyard of a house. The householder had a fierce cat. When the tailor-bird's eggs hatched into three chicks, the cat said: 'I want to eat those chicks.' He came and stood at the base of the tree, ready to climb into the nest.

The tailor-bird saw the cat, bowed her head and touched the branch.

'Humble greetings, your majesty,' she said. The cat was so pleased with this greeting that he walked away. The next day the cat came back and stood at the base of the tree looking hungrily up at the nest. Once again the tailor-bird treated the cat as if he were a king. The cat was so full of himself that he forgot about the chicks and walked away.

Day after day the same thing happened until one day the tailor-bird asked her chicks if they could fly to the roof of the house. 'We will try,' the chicks told her. They succeeded. When the cat came again and looked up at the nest the bird looked at him and said: 'Get lost, you big fool!'. The furious cat rushed up the tree and leapt for the nest. But the bird and her chicks flew away long before he reached it. The cat was left with nothing but his injured vanity.

Investigate

Aesop was probably one of the greatest writers of fables. Borrow a book of his *Fables* from your school or local library. Which fables do the common expressions 'sour grapes' and 'dog in the manger' come from? How many other well-used expressions can you find? What do they mean?

Another true story...

Stories which have a message have always been popular, and still are today. Read these two modern short stories and try to work out the message behind each one.

The unfortunate couple

There was a young couple who lived on a new housing estate. They were proud of their house and their car, and they kept both spick and span. They took the same train to work every morning, leaving the car parked outside their house. One morning, they opened the front door and stopped dead. Their car was missing! They rushed to the police station to report the theft. The police took down all the details and were sympathetic, but they were not hopeful.

When the couple eventually returned home from work, they ate a miserable supper and went to bed. The next morning they stepped out of the front door at exactly the same time. They stopped in amazement. The car was back. They walked all round it, looking carefully – there was not a scratch on it. Something had been left on the seat. It was a bottle of champagne, and with it was a letter. 'I am sorry I had to borrow your car,' it read. 'I am a doctor and it was an emergency. Please accept these two tickets to the theatre as compensation.'

The couple were delighted. They phoned the police and told them not to worry, as the car had been returned. That night they dressed up and went to the theatre. They thoroughly enjoyed themselves.

Afterwards, they were walking down their road hand in hand, when a feeling of dismay began to creep over them. They began to run. They reached their house and breathed a sigh of relief. The car was still there! They opened their front door and went inside. To their horror, they discovered that the house had been burgled. Everything that could be moved had been taken – even the rugs. Someone had obviously taken the time to do a thorough job – someone who knew they would be out all evening.

The mysterious hitch-hiker

A nun was driving through lonely countryside. It was raining and beginning to get dark. Suddenly she saw an old woman by the side of the road, holding her hand out as if she wanted a lift.

'I can't leave her out in this weather,' the nun said to herself. So she stopped the car and opened the door.

'Do you want a lift?' she asked. The old woman nodded and climbed into the car. After a while she said to the old woman, 'Have you been waiting long?' The old woman shook her head. 'Strange,' thought the nun. She tried again. 'Nasty weather for the time of year,' she said. The old woman nodded.

No matter what the nun said, the hitch-hiker gave no answer except for a nod of the head or a shrug. Then the nun noticed the hitch-hiker's hands, which were very large and hairy. Suddenly the nun realised that the hitch-hiker was really a man. She stopped the car. 'I can't see out of the rear windscreen,' she said. 'Would you be kind enough to clear it for me?' The hitch-hiker nodded and opened the door. As soon as the hitch-hiker was out of the car, the terrified nun raced off.

When the nun reached the next village, she pulled up. She noticed that the hitch-hiker had left her handbag behind. She picked it up and opened it. She gave a gasp. Inside the bag was a gun.

Stories like these are called **apocryphal stories**. They are told as if they are true, but no one really believes that they have actually happened. They are passed on from one person to the next, like a folk-tale. They even turn up in newspapers as if they have actually happened...

- They often take place in an obviously modern setting, for example in a car or a city.
- They often contain advice or messages for their listeners.
- They often appear to be true.

They are an example of the way in which language can be used to tell a story as well as to help us make sense of the world in which we live.

Gods, people and the supernatural

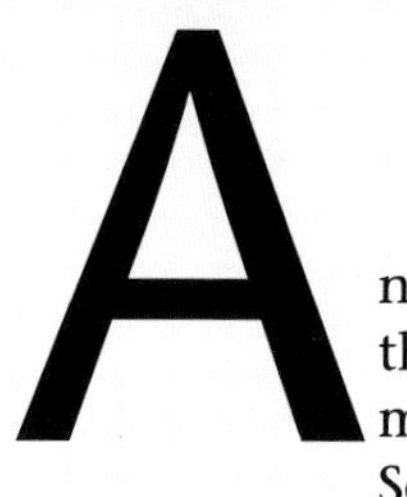

nother kind of story which has influenced the way we use words is the **myth**. A myth is a story which attempts to explain something mysterious, and normally involves supernatural happenings. Sometimes these stories have become so well known that phrases from them have entered everyday English.

THE MIDAS TOUCH

Golden Touch

Most people dream at some time of being rich. Read this famous myth about one man's experiences.

The golden touch

King Midas liked being rich. He liked living in a palace, having lots of servants, eating wonderful food and wearing fine clothes. He was lucky. He had everything he needed and more besides.

But that wasn't enough for him. Midas was greedy. He wanted to be even more wealthy. He dreamed of being the richest man who had ever lived. He began to be obsessed with gold. Nothing made him happier than running piles of golden coins through his fingers.

His wife looked on with growing concern. She tried to think of things to distract him, but nothing else kept his attention for very long. Soon he would stop listening to what was being said. Instead, he would sit back in his chair, and a distant look would come into his eyes as he began mentally counting up bag after bag of golden coins.

Despite his greed, Midas wasn't a bad person. He loved his family, especially his youngest daughter. She was his favourite.

He could be very kind to his friends, even to total strangers. In fact, it was his kindness that really caused his downfall. When an old man who seemed either lost or drunk, and possibly both, turned up at the door, the servants would have sent him packing immediately, but Midas felt sorry for him. He fed and clothed the old man and entertained him. Some of the servants thought it was a generous thing to do. Others muttered that it was just a way for Midas to show an old beggar what a rich man he was.

But the old man was no beggar. His name, when he could remember it the next morning, was Silenus. He was the foster-father of the god Dionysus, and a very important person, even if he did drink rather too much for his own good. When Dionysus heard how well Midas had treated the old man, he was very pleased. He decided to repay the king with equal generosity. He came down to Earth and found Midas walking in the countryside. He offered to grant the king any wish he named. 'But be careful,' Dionysus warned him. 'Think before you speak.

Thinking was not Midas's strong point. He did not hesitate for one moment. 'I wish that everything I touch would turn to gold,' he replied.

Dionysus shook his head in disbelief. The behaviour of mortals never ceased to amaze him. 'Very well,' he said with a sigh. 'Your wish is granted.' Then he disappeared.

Midas stood for a moment wondering if he had been dreaming. Hesitantly, he stuck out his hand and touched a leaf. It instantly turned to gold. Midas laughed out loud and ran around like a child. He touched twigs, stones, blades of grass. Everything turned to gold. He stuffed the glittering objects into his pockets and ran as fast as he could back to the palace.

His wife was alarmed to see him out of breath, but he could not wait to explain. He wanted to show her his wonderful gift. 'Look!' he told her. He seized a peach from a fruit bowl. The queen gave a gasp as it turned to gold in his hand. Midas put the peach down and rapidly touched the rest of the fruit.

'I've got the golden touch,' he told her. He walked about the room turning chairs, tables and cushions to gold.

Just then his youngest daughter rushed into the room. 'Daddy!' she cried and she ran towards him.

'Stop!' the queen shrieked, but it was too late. The moment the child touched her father she was frozen into a golden statue, beautiful but lifeless, poised with her hands raised up to her father. Midas looked at the child and his joy turned to horror. He realised at last what a dreadful mistake he had made.

Activity

What do you think this myth tells us about:

a gold
b being able to wish for anything you want
c thinking
d being kind to people?

Investigate

Find out where the following expressions come from:

Trojan horse
Achilles heel
carrying the world on your shoulders

How many other myths do you know? Which countries do they come from? Have any of them led to English expressions which you use?

Nursery rhymes

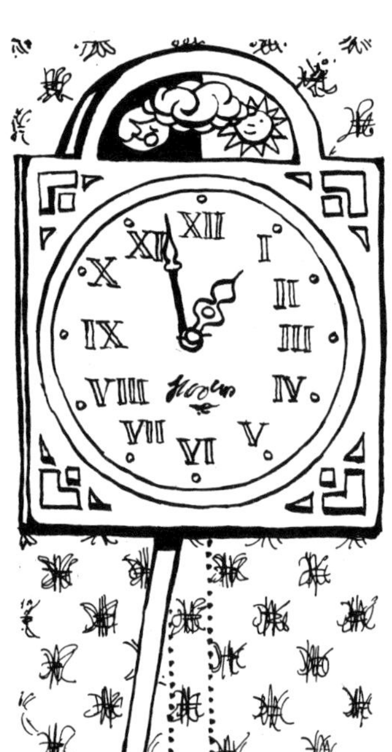

Hickory dickory dock
The mouse ran up the clock
The clock struck one
The mouse fell down
Hickory dickory dock.

Sat little Renu with a bowl hearty,
Full of buttered, sugared chappati,
Suddenly a tiny mouse appeared,
Frightening little Renu dear,
Aside was flung the bowl hearty,
Full of buttered, sugared chappati.

ਥਾਲੀ ਵਿੱਚ ਰੱਖ ਮਖਣ ਰੋਟੀ
ਖਾਣ ਬੈਠੀ ਰੇਨੂੰ ਛੋਟੀ।
ਇਨੇ ਵਿੱਚ ਚੂਹੀ ਇਕ ਆਈ
ਉਹਨੂੰ ਵੇਖ ਰੇਨੂੰ ਘਬਰਾਈ।
ਫਿਰ ਕੀ ਸੀ ਬੱਸ ਸੁਟ ਦਿਤੀ ਥਾਲੀ
ਮੱਖਣ ਰੋਟੀ ਚੀਨੀ ਵਾਲੀ।

The first stories that most of us experience are the nursery rhymes we learn when we are very young. It is no accident that these are called 'rhymes'. 'Dock' sounds similar to 'clock': it rhymes. When a word or part of a word ends in the same sound as another it is said to **rhyme**.

At first, very young children are more interested in the sounds of words than in what the words mean. As they learn what words mean, they still like the way they sound, and often find it easier to remember words which sound similar.

Nursery rhymes also tend to have a strong **rhythm**, a regular beat. It means that parts of words are particularly stressed in any one line. All groups of words have rhythm, but in nursery rhymes the rhythm is often deliberately simple and strong.

Activity

In pairs, read *Hickory dickory dock* aloud. Which parts of which words do you stress when you say it? What is the rhythm of the words meant to suggest? How many of the words in this rhyme are real ones?

The nursery rhymes which children learn are full of made-up words as well as real ones. For example 'dickory' and 'dock'. Some people think that these words are old words for numbers. This is because in some areas of the country there are special counting words used by shepherds, fishermen and knitters which contain words similar to these. It is also thought that counting rhymes using numbers like these were used by the Ancient Druids when they were choosing human sacrifices.

Look at this chart showing different ways of counting to ten. If you read each set of numbers aloud, you will see how strong the rhythm is.

Oral numerals

West Riding, Yorkshire	Yarmouth	Northumberland	Westmorland	North Riding, Yorkshire
eina	ina	een	yan	yan
peina	mina	tean	tyan	tean
paira	tethera	tether	tethera	tithera
puttera	methera	mether	methera	mithera
pith	pin	pimp	pimp	mimph
ith	sithera	citer	sethera	hitter
awith	lithera	liter	lethera	litter
air-a	cothra	ova	hevera	over
dickala	hothra	dova	devera	dover
dick	dic	dic	dick	dick

Even modern counting rhymes can have a sense of the unpleasant about them:

Ippa dippa dation
My operation
How many people
Waiting at the station?

Ding dong bell,
Pussy's in the well.
Who put her in?
Little Tommy Thin.

Activity

Do you know any counting, dipping or choosing rhymes like the ones above? If so, tell them to the rest of your class and then write them down.

Investigate

Look for other nursery rhymes which seem to have a nasty message or are connected in some way with death. There will be plenty of examples in the young children's section of your local library. Why do you think children like rhymes such as these? Why do you think nursery rhymes contain so many nonsense words and ideas?

five ONCE UPON A TIME

Starting point

Wherever English is spoken, its alphabet is of great importance. Without an agreed set of letters it would be impossible to write anything which could be read and understood by other English speakers.

Learning the names of all twenty-six letters, how they can sound and how to write a small and large version of them is something which all English-speaking children need to do.

- All letters have two different forms. We call these **upper case** and **lower case**, or **capital letter** and **small letter**.
- A few capital letters look the same as their small versions (for example 'c' and 'C'). Most look different (for example 'b' and 'B').
- Sometimes a letter is typed differently from the way it is written (for example 'ɑ' and 'a').
- Capitals are used for the first letter of proper names, like 'Elizabeth' or for the first letter of a new sentence. Some languages use capitals differently. If you have studied German, you will know that a capital letter is used for the first letter of all nouns.

Although there are two basic forms of each letter, all letters can be represented in a variety of ways on paper. The different sizes and designs of letters are known as **typography**.

A Serif typeface

A Serif typeface in bold

A Serif typeface in italics

A sans serif typeface

A sans serif typeface in bold

A sans serif typeface in italics

Outline **Shadow** **Reverse**

Different **typefaces**.

Investigate

Collect as many different examples of typography as you can. Choose one word and show by copying or cutting out examples how each letter of the word varies in different typefaces. Which typeface do you prefer? Why?

How the alphabet developed

obody knows exactly how or when writing started. Examples of a kind of writing have been found in the Middle East and south-east Europe on clay tablets which date back to 3500 BC. It seems likely that the first attempts at writing were more like pictures.

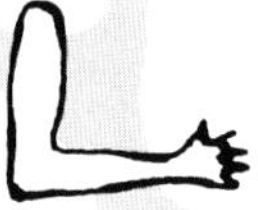

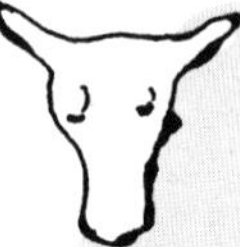

These pictures are called **pictograms**. 'Pictogram' means 'painted writing' from the Latin word *pingere*, 'to paint', and the Greek word, *gramma*, meaning 'written'.

Activity

Pictograms are still widely used throughout the world. How many of these do you recognise?

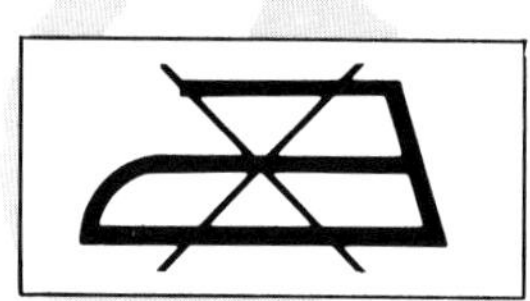

Investigate

Do you know any other pictograms? Make up some of your own. Draw a poster, only made up of pictograms, on which you try and put across a clear message without using any words.

From Phoenician to English

Using letters to show sounds isn't actually the most obvious way of communicating in writing. Early written symbols usually stood for ideas or a series of ideas, like the Egyptian sign ⊙ which can mean 'sun', 'god' or 'daytime'.

A system which uses letters to represent sounds is called **alphabetic**, after *alpha* and *beta*, the first two letters of the Ancient Greek alphabet. The earliest known alphabet was the North Semitic one, which developed in Palestine and Syria around 1700 BC. The Phoenician alphabet was based on this and the Greeks based their alphabet on the Phoenician one. The Etruscans used the Greek alphabet as a model and the Romans used the Etruscan. The English alphabet is essentially Roman with a few modifications.

This chart shows how the different letters have developed into the ones we use today.

hieroglyph Eygpt	sound value	meaning	Phoenician 1300 BC	Greek 500 BC	Roman AD 100
	ah	ox		A	A
	per	house		B	B
	teba	finger		Γ	G
	seb	door		Δ	D
		man		E	E
	d	hand		Δ	D
	ee			I	I
	k	vessel		K	K
	n	water		M	M
	ch	serpent		N	N
	r	mouth		Π	P
	k,g	pot		Γ	C
	f	sérpent		Y	F
	sh	field		Σ	S
	m	owl		M	M
	ari	eye		O	O
	q	angle			Q
	tep	head		P	R
	l, r	lion		Λ	L
	s	?		Ξ	X
		to be in		T	T

Activity

Find out if there are any members of your class who can also recognise another alphabet. Get them to tell you how it is different from the English one.

Investigate

Find out about other alphabets like the ones used in braille, in sign language, Morse code and semaphore. What special features does each one have? Who are they designed for?

Putting it in words of one syllable

The English alphabet we use today has twenty-six letters. There are two kinds of letters, called **vowels** and **consonants**. The vowels are the letters 'a', 'e', 'i', 'o' and 'u'. All the rest are consonants, although the letter 'y' is sometimes used as a vowel.

All words can be broken down into small parts called **syllables**. A syllable is made up of a mixture of consonants and vowels, for example:

'catastrophe' has four syllables:
ca–ta–stro–phe
'invent' has two syllables:
in–vent
'was' has only one syllable

The easiest way of being sure how many syllables there are in a word is by saying the word out loud. Imagine you are chanting it at a football match, like 'Li–ver–pool'.

Activity

Turn back to page 90. In pairs, read some of the nursery rhymes out loud. How many syllables are there in each word? How many words are there with more than three syllables in them?

Look at a piece of your own writing. How many syllables are there in most of your words?

Look at any page in a dictionary. Which word has the most syllables? How many does it have?

Vowels and consonants do different jobs in the syllables they make up. Vowels are more often found in the middle of syllables, like the 'a' in 'ca' at the beginning of 'catastrophe', or the 'e' in 'vent' at the end of 'invent'.

However, this is not always true. 'I' is a vowel, but it occurs at the beginning of the first syllable of 'invent'.

Consonants are more often found at the beginning and end of words, like the 'n' and 't' at the end of 'invent'.

Another difference between vowels and consonants is in the way we say them. The sound of a vowel is made differently from that of a consonant. If you say the letters 'a', 'e', 'i', 'o' and 'u' slowly to yourself and then say some of the other letters, you will see that the vowel sounds are made with an open mouth, whereas the consonant sounds are made with the mouth partially closed.

Although there are twenty-six letters in the English alphabet, some are used more frequently than others. The vowel 'e' is the most common letter, followed by the consonant 't'.

Activity

Count up the letters on a page of a book you are reading. Compare your results with a partner's. Add them up together. See if 'e' and 't' are the most common. Which letters are the third and fourth most common? Compare your findings with the rest of the class. Did you all get the same results?

Investigate

Find out about the Morse code. Why do you think it was important for Samuel Morse (1791–1872) to know which letters were most commonly used when he invented the code?

Look at the letters opposite from the game *Scrabble*. From the number value given to the letters, can you work out a rank order for the most commonly used letters in the alphabet?

A Morse code operator.

Some words, like some letters, are used more often than others. As a general rule the longer a word is, the less often it is used.

Activity

Which words do you use most? Do the same count as the one you did on letters. Look at:

- **a** your own writing
- **b** a newspaper
- **c** writing from an author you like

Are there any differences? Why? What do you think the ten most commonly used words are? (Look at the list in the box on page 98.)

It has been worked out that in 96% of conversations we use 737 words. Shakespeare used more than thirty thousand words in his plays, but a typical person today uses nothing like this many words.

Some people measure the length and number of words to help them to identify old manuscripts. When there was a dispute about whether Francis Bacon or William Shakespeare wrote all those famous plays, the methods of forensic science were applied. By comparing the plays with other pieces of writing known to have been produced by Bacon and Shakespeare it was found that there were more four-letter words than three-letter ones in Shakespeare, whereas the opposite was the case in Bacon's writing. Bacon also used more long words. On this evidence, Shakespeare is the author of the plays.

By William Shakespeare.

Actus primus, Scena prima.

A tempeſtuous noiſe of Thunder and Lightning heard: Enter a Ship-maſter, and a Boteſwaine.

Maſter.

Bote-ſwaine.

By Francis Bacon.

ons, & haue in themſelues the foreſight of Immortalitie, in their deſcendents, ſhould likewiſe be more carefull of the good eſtate of future times; vnto which they know they muſt tranſmitte and commend ouer their dearreſt pledges. Queene *Elizabeth* was a ſoiourner in the world in reſpect of her vnmaried life: and was

The challenge of spelling

You have already learned how English developed so that words are spelled as they are today. With the influence of French and Latin and the decisions taken by printers and dictionary-makers, there are many accepted spellings which do not seem to make much sense today.

Autumn eye listen shoulder young
cough lamb quay women

Activity

Copy them out and mark any letters which:

a appear in the word but are not pronounced

b appear in the word but are pronounced in a way that is different from what you would have expected.

The Simplified Spelling Society

The Simplified Spelling Society is an organisation which is trying to change our writing system by 'modernising' the spelling of English. The Society believes that now that English has become an international language, it is time to reform its spelling because it is so difficult and illogical.

The Simplified Spelling Society points out how difficult it is to teach spelling to a five-year-old. Look at these examples: 'bun', 'mother', 'wonder', 'thunder'. Why are some spelled with a 'u' and some with an 'o'? In the Society's view, they should be spelled: 'bun', 'muther', 'wunder', 'thunder'.

The problem is that there are only five written vowels in English – a e i o u – but many more spoken vowels than can be covered by these letters. So, 'a' in 'fat', 'fate', 'call', 'father' and 'soap' has a different sound in each case.

For this reason the Society has made up a **phonetic** alphabet, that is to say an alphabet based on the way letters sound when they are spoken in an agreed way. If you look at most dictionaries, you will see that such alphabets already exist and are used to help you see how a word is pronounced in Standard English.

Written English	Spoken English
1 the	1 the
2 of	2 and
3 to	3 I
4 in	4 to
5 and	5 of
6 a	6 a
7 for	7 you
8 was	8 that
9 is	9 in
10 that	10 it

To make this phonetic alphabet, the Society has changed the English alphabet in a number of ways. The most obvious change is to the vowels. At the moment there is a problem about the 'a' in 'm**a**t' and the 'a' in 'm**a**te'. One is short and the other long in sound, but they are both written as 'a'. In the simplified spelling, 'mate' would be spelled 'maet', making it clear that the 'a' was long.

This works for all the other vowels except 'i', so that there are four new letters: 'ae', 'ee', 'oe' and 'ue'. For 'i', 'y' is used for the long 'i' sound in '**by**' and 'i' for the short 'i' sound in 'p**i**t'.

Activity

This short story, by H. G. Wells, appeared with the author's permission in 1942. Can you understand it? Read it aloud in groups.

The star

It woz on the ferst dae ov the nue yeer that the anounsment woz maed, aulmoest simultaeneusli from three obzervatoris, that the moeshen ov the planet Neptune, the outermoest ov aul the planets that w(h)eel about the sun, had bekum veri eratik. A retardaeshen in its velositi had been suspekted in Desember. Then a faent, remoet spek ov lyt woz diskuverd in the reejen ov the perterbd planet. At ferst this did not kauz eni veri graet eksytment. Syentifik peepl, houever, found the intelijens remarkabl enuf, eeven befor it bekaem noen that the nue bodi woz rapidli groeing larjer and bryter, and that its moeshen woz kwyt diferent from the orderli proegres ov the planets...

On the therd dae ov the nue yeer the nuespaeper reeders ov too hemisfeers wer maed awaer for the ferst tym ov the real importens ov this unuezhueal aparishen in the hevens. 'A Planetari Kolizhen' wun London paeper heded the nues, and proklaemd that this straenj planet wood probabli kolyd with Neptune. The leeder-ryters enlarjd upon the topik. So that in moest ov the kapitals ov the werld, on Janueari 3rd, thaer woz an ekspektaeshen, houever vaeg, ov sum iminent fenomenen in the sky; and az the nyt foloed the sunset round the gloeb, thouzends ov men ternd thaer ys skywerd to see–the oeld familier stars just az thae had aulwaez been.

Until it woz daun in London and the stars oeverhed had groen pael. The winter's daun it woz, a sikli, filtering akuemuelashen ov daelyt, and the lyt ov gas and kandls shon yeloe in the windoes to shoe w(h)aer peepl wer astur. But the yauning poleesman sau the thing, the bizi krouds in the markets stopt agaep, werkmen goeing to thaer werk betymz, milkmen, Disipaeshen goeing hoem jaeded and pael, hoemles wonderers, and, in the kuntri, laeberers trujing afeeld, poechers slinking hoem, and oever the duski kwikening kuntri it kood be seen – and out at see by seemen woching for the dae – a graet w(h)yt star, kum sudenli into the westwerd sky!

Bryter it woz than eni star in our skys: bryter than the eevning star at its brytest. It stil gloed out w(h)yt and larj, noe meer twinkling spot ov lyt, but a smaul, round, kleer shyning disk, an our after the dae had kum. And w(h)aer syens haz not reecht, men staerd and feerd, teling wun anuther ov the wors and pestilenses that ar forshadoed by theez fyri syns in the hevens.

And in a hundred obzervatoris thaer had been suprest eksytment, ryzing aulmoest to shouting pich, az the too remoet bodis had rusht together, and a huriing to and froe, to gather foetografik aparaetus and spektroskoep, and this aplyens and that, to rekord this novel, astonishing syt, the destrukshen ov a werld.

Understanding sentences

You have already found out about how printers developed a number of punctuation marks to make sense of printed English. You have also come across sentences, although you may feel unsure about how to define what a sentence is.

Here are some attempts at defining a sentence:

1. A sentence is the complete expression of a thought. For example, 'I had a great weekend.'
2. A sentence is a group of words which make complete sense, for example 'I went into town yesterday.', rather than 'I went into'.
3. A sentence needs to have a subject to make complete sense, for example 'Thomas put his book on the table.', rather than 'put his book on the table'.
4. A sentence needs to have a verb, for example 'This is what I'm trying to tell you.', rather than 'Eighty-three years'.
5. A sentence must start with a capital letter and end with a full stop, exclamation mark or question mark.

In pairs, read the following extract carefully. It is taken from the beginning of *New Guys Around the Block* by Rosa Guy.

> Packed together, they pushed, shoved, straining toward the round spot of light – and escape. Blocking their retreat, the shadow stretched out over them, threatening oblivion. They squeezed, clawed, fought each other, stampeding forward. Neck to neck, fur brushing fur, bodies glistening in the wild scramble.
>
> Rats! Hundreds and hundreds of rats! Rats locked together in a frenzied struggle – mindless, snapping, desperate. And he was one of them. He could see his eyes. They were intelligent. He didn't belong. Opening his mouth he shouted, *'Squeak, squeak, squeak.'* His back bristled – and then he fought. Fighting the pack, fighting to move backward, fighting to stand still... Digging his claws into the wood of the floor, he cowered, still resisting the mob. But the surge of terrified gray bodies kept pushing, sweeping him along.

Intelligently, he began to maneuver forward. He shouldered his way, first past one, then another, burrowing through one group, then another. And he made it. Haloed by the spot of light, he jumped – into space!

Floating down, his paws clawing the air, bodies falling on either side of him, he looked down. Water raged below, beating against jagged rocks on which hundreds of gray, furry cadavers had already been pierced, blood darkening the water...

Jumping out of bed in the hot room, Imamu switched on the light at the side of his bed and rushed to the dresser. Staring into the mirror, he ran his hands over his face. Yes, he still stood six feet two, smooth, black, and slender. His Afro haircut, matted down from sleep, made a crown around his head – rough, instead of slick to the touch. He pinched his nose; it was high, broad instead of pointed. And his hands – praise the Lord – were still large, the fingers long. 'Imamu Jones, you're still a human goddamn being...'

He sat at the edge of his bed, fighting for control. Picking up a soiled shirt from the chair next to the bed, he wiped the sweat from his clammy body. The clock on the dresser pointed to five-thirty. Easing away from the cold spot of his sweat, Imamu got back into bed. 'Imamu Jones,' he whispered, 'what in the world did you do to earn yourself that nightmare, man?' He lay staring up at the ceiling, at the paint curling as though ready to fall on him.

He turned his eyes to the window, looked long and hard at the torn shade, the dirty curtains, then at the walls – gray from years of neglect, the cracked plaster spilling fine dust over the floors. He gazed at the black finger marks around the doorknob. And all through the house it was the same – the kitchen, its walls thick with grease; the bathroom a nightmare of peeling ceiling and walls; his mother's bedroom, the hallway, crying out for paint...

Activity

Read this extract again carefully. How many of Rosa Guy's sentences do not appear to obey any of the definitions given on page 100? Does definition number 5 apply to all her sentences? Do all her sentences have verbs?

More about sentences

When you are speaking you do not produce a continuous stream of words. You leave short gaps in what you are saying. This is because we tend to construct our speech in sections.

Speaking in sections like this is not something we do consciously. It allows you to get your breath. It also prevents you from confusing the person you are talking to although, of course, there are some people who go on and on as if they are never going to stop.

When you write, it is also necessary to break your words into groups. Many people think that all writing should be divided up clearly into sentences, or else it is incorrect. However, you have seen from the extract on pages 100–1 that there are a large number of ways in which these gaps between words can be dealt with. For example, words like 'Yes', 'Happy birthday', 'Hello', 'Good evening' often appear as sentences.

You have already seen how the so-called rule that a sentence must start with a capital letter and end with a full stop, exclamation mark or question mark is not always followed by respected writers today. However, it is still important to know exactly what you are doing when you construct and punctuate groups of words. When a writer deliberately chooses to avoid the normal accepted sentence construction, there is usually a very good reason for it.

Read this extract from the beginning of *Isaac Campion*, by Janni Howker. You will see that, to create almost a conversational feel to the book, Janni Howker uses sentences in very interesting ways.

Now then, I was twelve, rising thirteen, when our Daniel got killed. Aye... it was a long time ago. I'm talking about a time of day eighty-three years back. Eighty-three years. It's a time of day that's past your imagining. I'm talking about a different world. You might as well say it was a different planet, the world I was born in.

No radios. No televisions. No World Wars. They'd not even built the *Titanic*, let alone sunk her. This is it, you see. This is what I'm trying to tell you. When you look back over all those years, you think that what happened was bound to happen. You can't imagine that it could happen any different.

They've got this notion about the past, about history – they forget that folks lived in it – well, we didn't know what was going to happen. It's the same for the young ones, they think they are going to live forever. And good luck to them, I say! Good luck to the young ones, let them live to ninety-six! Let them live to a hundred!

Eighty-three years back... It's me that should be dead and buried in my grave, but I'm telling you, I can remember the day Dan died just as clear as *that*!

There's me and Joe Flitch, the clogger's son, crouched in this muddy little drainage ditch behind the schoolhouse on Chapel Street. Stinker Beck, we called it.

Crouched in the smelly yellow mud, we were, where no one could see us.

'Go on,' I says to Joe. 'Go on. I dare thee! Eat one!' I was egging him on, you see.

We'd been let out of the school-room after a day of chanting times-tables and 'Twelve inches make a foot. Three feet make a yard...' with tall Miss Whitehead glaring down at us like the eye of God! She was a terror, was that schoolmistress. We were all scared of her.

But she couldn't see us in the ditch. 'Go on!' I says to Joe. Just to see if he would. Poor Mazey Joe starts sniggling and snorting. He wasn't right in the head. He wasn't the full shilling. We were always daring him to do daft things. The pleasure wasn't in teasing him. Teasing Joe Flitch was too easy. No. I'd say the pleasure was in thinking up something crackers enough for him to do so's you could tell tales about it afterwards.

'Ah can, Isaac! Ah can eat 'em!' he kept spluttering. 'Ah swallered a clog nail once.'

I can just see him – crouched in the mud like a fledgeling that's fallen out of a nest, with his tuft of hair bristling on his head, and his thin elbows and knees poking out of his clothes. Spitting and giggling.

I was watching the water dripping between his fingers, and these two tadpoles were wriggling and stranded in his hand. Well, I didn't really believe that even Mazey Joe Flitch was daft enough to eat a tadpole.

I should have known better.

'Oh, put 'em back,' I says. It was giving me knee-ache, squatting there, and anyway I wanted to go and meet our Daniel outside *The Bear and Staff*. So I was just going to reach out and knock the tadpoles off his hand and back into the ditch, when Joe suddenly stops giggling, claps his hand to his mouth and sucks!

'Bloody goomer!' I jumped up, yelling at him to spit them out. Well, it made me feel sick to my belly. Oh, it was my fault for daring him to do it, but that didn't stop me feeling sick at the sight. 'Yer goomer! Spit 'em out! They'll grow into frogs inside thee and tha'll die!'

Aye! That's how we talked at each other in them days – right harsh. Right broad speech, as you might say. I couldn't have understood a man from London, and he'd not have understood me.

Any road, Joe Flitch was as simple as a smack on the head, and he just laughs and says, 'Ah can eat ants an' all, Isaac!' That's what he says! 'Ah can eat ants an' all!' And he's grinning all over his thin little face...

Eighty-odd years ago... And there's me scrambling out of the ditch, feeling sick to me guts. But that afternoon was only beginning. April 17th 1901... That was the day of our Dan's death... That day's fixed in my mind like a picture. Do you know something? I can even smell that day...

This is the only way we have, you see, to go back into the past. This business of remembering. But it is false. You can't go back because you know what is going to happen. But you didn't know what was going to happen then, you see? You did not know. You are just living your life, wondering what it is all about. You don't know what might be important. You don't know anything.

And that's how it was. There's me, off like a shot, scrambling over the school-yard wall and jumping down into the cobbled street. It was all cobbles then, or setts, and that's a bad surface for running on. I could hear Mazey Joe clattering after us in his heavy clogs, with his skinny legs going like a pair of scissors, but I didn't want him near me. Oh no. Not bloody likely! Not after he'd done that. Well, I shot round the corner of Chapel Street and nearly bolted a hitch of dray horses outside *The Turk's Head*. But when I looked back to see if he was catching up, Joe had stopped to watch the fellers rolling the beer barrels off the cart and into the cellar. They used to make a lovely soft thundery sound, those wooden casks, when they were rolled across cobbles.

Activity

What are the most obvious features of Janni Howker's sentences? Make a list of them. Does she follow any of the definitions given on page 100? Write a story of your own in which you deliberately explore different types of sentence.

Points to remember

Sentences are the basic unit of all stories. Even the simplest of descriptions of a sentence can be misleading. Nevertheless, most sentences do start with a capital letter and end with a full stop, an exclamation mark or a question mark. They also make sense in that words appear in a certain order ('I went into town yesterday.' not 'Town went I yesterday into.). Most sentences also have a subject and a verb. The subject of a sentence is the person or thing that does what the verb describes ('**I** (subject) **went** (verb) into town yesterday.').

Simile and metaphor in literature

When authors want to bring their writing alive they often do more than just describe what they are writing about. They use their imagination and introduce a comparison which sparks off all sorts of ideas in the mind of their readers.

Activity

Read this extract. It is the opening of a novel by Nina Bawden called *Carrie's War.*

> Carrie had often dreamed about coming back. In her dreams she was twelve years old again; short, scratched legs in red socks and scuffed, brown sandals, walking along the narrow, dirt path at the side of the railway line to where it plunged down, off the high ridge, through the Druid's Grove. The yew trees in the Grove were dark green and so old that they had grown twisted and lumpy, like arthritic fingers. And in Carrie's dream, the fingers reached out for her, plucking at her hair and her skirt as she ran. She was always running by the end of this dream, running away from the house, uphill towards the railway line.

The phrase 'they had grown twisted and lumpy, like arthritic fingers' is a **simile**. A simile is a type of description in which one thing is likened to another using the word 'like' or 'as'. In this phrase the yew trees come alive as lumpy and threatening fingers ready to touch Carrie.

Comparisons which use 'like' or 'as' are easily noticed. However, writers sometimes choose to make comparisons in slightly less obvious ways.

Read these two extracts taken from *The Catalogue of the Universe* by Margaret Mahy. In both of them there is a simile, but there is also another kind of comparison which is not signposted quite so clearly.

Tyco was not used to being alone. Silence took him by surprise, and he found himself walking down the hall looking past open doors into rooms made unfamiliar by quietness. The silent house seemed engaged in a secret debate of its own for, without its people, everything in it – his father's worn slippers under a chair; Richard's camera watching him like an eye from the hall table; his mother's apron, a discarded floral skin hanging on the back of the kitchen door – all took on new meanings. In his own room the walls around his bed now sang to him like a chorus of actual voices and although he was not exactly comforted, he was certainly sustained by their sympathy. They suggested that the true beauty of the world lay in its mystery, which, however, men must struggle to understand.

* * *

Angela and Dido lived in a house which Dido was slowly buying, at the top of Dry Creek Road, a road rooted down in the city, but climbing up over the hills, increasingly jostled by wild flowers, weeds, long grasses and golden broom, until all houses stopped. The blue-black asphalt ended with them, and Dry Creek Road became more of a track, in spite of its proud name. As it climbed, it began to swoop and curve, writhing like a desperate serpent pinned down and anxious to be free. A sturdy bridge crossed the great, branching scar of the dry creek from which the road took its name – a creek of barren stones, capable of bearing, after a night of rain, a swollen torrent that would roar like a beast on a continual, angry note as if the hillside itself had found a throat and was issuing a warning. Up above the bridge the road grew leaner and more treacherous, held at bay on one side by a bank alive with moss and ferns and broom and foxgloves, while on the other it surrendered to the void, a great airy fall on to stony slopes far below. Not only this, the road claimed victims just as if it were a serpent god. Hedgehogs, possums, magpies and rabbits were killed by cars, particularly close to the city, for nobody lived near the top except Dido and Angela May, and a morose farmer with the cheerful name of Charlie Cherry. He had two sons, Phil and Jerry Cherry, who often drove by Angela and Dido on the way home, burning past them even on corners, blasting the horn at them contemptuous of their slow and careful descent.

'Silence took him by surprise' and 'a road rooted down in the city, but climbing up over the hills, increasingly jostled by wild flowers' are examples of **metaphor**. A metaphor is a kind of comparison. Unlike a simile, it does not use 'like' or 'as'. It just describes something as if it were something else. Here, silence is described as if it were a person. (In fact, this kind of metaphor is called a **personification** because of this.) The road is like a plant 'rooted' to the city. The wild flowers do not actually jostle the road, but they are described as if they do.

Activity

As you continue through your current reading book, note down examples of similes and metaphors. How effective do you think they are? Try including these descriptive techniques in your own writing.

Understanding tense

Armed raiders **escaped** with ten thousand pounds.

She **goes** to the new school.

When you read newspapers or listen to the news, you will notice that most of the verbs are in the past tense (for example 'escap**ed**' not 'escape'). When you listen to a sports commentary on television, it is often in the present tense (for example 'is' not 'was').

Writers of stories can use any tense, although normally they choose either the present or the past. The tense they choose does affect the way the language works and you need to be aware that this is a decision that you take every time you write.

Look at these two versions of a very short story.

Dino's headache

1

I wake up out of a dream about my mother. I try hard to stay asleep. I want to be back in the dream. I want to be at home, talking to my mother. But it's no good. I have to wake up. The room is exactly the same as before: bare walls, a bare light bulb, a table and a chair, a mattress which I have been lying on. Nothing else.

I get up, walk over to the door and try the handle. It is still locked. I rattle the handle and call out, 'Is anybody there?' My voice sounds weak and pathetic. I go back to the mattress and lie down. I have to think.

I decide that if I make a really loud noise someone might come. I pick up the chair with both hands and bring it down on the table with all my strength. Then I start shouting. I do this over and over again until two things happen: first the chair breaks and I am left holding one chair-leg; second the door bursts open. A huge, ugly man rushes in.

I am more scared than I have ever been in my life. I know I have just one chance. As the man walks towards me, I swing the leg of the chair and hit him on the side of the head. He yells and staggers backwards. I run out of the open door.

In front of me is a narrow hallway. At the end of it is another door. I race down the hallway. My heart feels like it is going to explode. I fumble with the door-catch, finally get it open. I am in a block of flats. The lift is right in front of me. The lift doors are open. I am too frightened to get in the lift. I start running down the stairs.

The man comes out of the door of the flat. He sees me and shouts something. I know he will kill me if he catches me. I keep running. My breath is like sandpaper in my chest.

2

Dino was on duty when it happened. The kid started screaming and smashing the place up. 'Dumb kid,' Dino muttered to himself. He went to try and quieten the kid down. As soon as he got inside the room the kid hit him with a chair-leg and ran out of the door. He went out the front door and ran down the steps.

Dino kept with him the whole time but the kid could really run. He went down seven flights of steps and out into the street. It was about four in the morning and there was no one about. The kid didn't know what time it was. He got a shock when he saw the empty streets. He looked around in every direction and then started running again.

That was when Dino made his second big mistake. He headed for the car. He should have just kept running after the kid but Dino had drunk too many beers the night before. His legs felt like lead after running down seven flights of stairs. Dino wasn't too good at thinking, but the way he had it figured was simple. The kid was on foot. Dino was in a car. It was no contest.

The kid heard Dino starting the engine. He looked back over his shoulder and saw the bright red car reversing out of its parking space. He stopped dead for a minute, looked around him.

Across the road was a children's playground, with swings, roundabouts and grass. The kid saw the playground and his eyes lit up. He raced across and climbed over the railings.

It took Dino a while to realise what the kid was doing. When he did he swore loudly and slammed on the brakes. By the time he had stopped the car, got out and climbed over the railings, he had lost sight of the kid altogether.

For the first time Dino stopped thinking about the kid. He started to think about himself. He was in trouble. He had let the kid go. He had let a quarter of a million pounds in ransom money hit him over the head and run out of the flat. Now, that quarter of a million was hiding somewhere in the park. Dino had to find it quick before people started appearing. His head was really starting to hurt. Maybe the kid wasn't so dumb, after all.

The story is told from two different points of view: the boy's and Dino's. The boy tells his own story using 'I' to describe himself. Dino's story is told for him by a narrator, using 'he' to describe Dino. But there is also a difference in tense. The boy says:

I wake up I get up I decide	} All of these are in the present tense.

However, in Dino's story the narrator says:

Dino was on duty he swore loudly Dino stopped thinking about the kid	} All of these are in the past tense.

Activity

Which of these two versions do you think grabs your attention more? Which seems more exciting? Which tense is it written in? Work out the key events of a short story of your own involving a kidnap. Tell it in both the present and the past tense. Read the stories written by other members of your group. Can you make any general comments about how different tenses affect your reactions to a story?

Person in stories

You will probably have noticed that the books you read are also written from different points of view. For example, you may read a sentence which says:

a 'I woke up as soon as my alarm clock rang.'
or
b 'He woke up as soon as his alarm clock rang.'

'Woke up' is a verb (see page 30). A verb is a word which describes an action. The point of view from which the action takes place is called its **person**. There are six possible points of view or persons that a verb can have in English.

We call example **a** a sentence in the **first person singular**. We call example **b** a sentence in the **third person singular**. The full list of persons in English is:

1st person singular	I
2nd person singular	you
3rd person singular	he, she or it
1st person plural	we
2nd person plural	you (more than one of you)
3rd person plural	they

Notice that the second person plural is the same as the second person singular. This is because we can use the word 'you' to mean one person or a group of people. In many other languages, however, they are different. The person that a writer chooses to use affects the way readers understand the story.

Read these two versions of the same story.

How to be a success

I knew it was going to work as soon as I woke up. Don't ask me how I knew. I just did. Most mornings, when my mum tells me it's time to get up, I feel like it can't possibly be time to wake up. I lie there thinking, 'No, it's still night time. Go away.' Not this morning. This morning I woke up feeling lucky. This was going to be my day. So when my mum knocked on the door and called out, 'Damian, it's half past seven,' I just shouted back, 'Right' and sprang out of bed.

'You're bright and breezy this morning,' my mum said when I got downstairs.

'It's a lovely day,' I told her.

'Is it?' she asked.

I felt sorry for her. She didn't know what it was like to feel lucky. Every day was the same for her: get up with my dad, see him off to work, make breakfast, see me off to school, go to work herself, come home, make dinner, go to bed. Nothing ever changed for her. But for me something was about to change. Today was the day I had been waiting for.

'I feel confident. I can do anything I want to. I am full of confidence, like a tiger ready to spring.' This was what I was saying to myself as I walked down the road towards the bus stop.

'The secret of success is confidence.' That was what the book said on the first page and I believed it.

'All you have to do is decide what it is you want. Then turn your whole mind towards achieving it.' That was how it went on. I had done just that. I knew exactly what I wanted and I was going to get it. I had turned my whole mind towards achieving my goal and I could feel it was working.

Before I had sent off for the book, *How to be a success*, I was miserable. I used to go around with drooping shoulders, staring at the pavement. Damian Stanhope was my name. People at school called me Damian No-hope. But not for very much longer they wouldn't.

'In order to feel confident, you should walk confidently,' the book suggested. That was good advice. Now I threw my shoulders back and held my head up. I looked the world in the eye.

£12.50 was a lot of money to pay for a book, but I reckoned it was worth it, even if it wasn't very thick. It had changed my life. Before reading it I had not had the courage to do the one thing that mattered to me. Since reading it I had grown braver and stronger every day. Today I knew it was all going to pay off. I could feel the blood pulsing in my veins as I walked down the road. Today I had the courage and I was going to do it. I was going to walk up to the girl at the bus stop and I was going to ask her out on a date.

I turned the corner. There, at the end of the road was the bus stop and there was the girl. As soon as I saw her I stopped dead. All the confidence, all the courage began to drain away from me.

'I can't do it,' I said to myself.

I stood outside the newsagent's shop, trying to decide what to do. I pretended to stare into the window but I kept looking at the bus stop. I had to do it. Today was my lucky day. But I couldn't do it.

I looked at my watch. In six minutes' time the 108b bus would come lumbering up to the stop. The automatic doors would open with a hiss of air. She would get on and I would not. I would stand there, waiting for the 123, watching my opportunity driving away, Damian No-hope.

'No!' I said to myself. I clenched my fists. What was it the book said? 'Courage is not a gift that some people have and others do not. It is an attitude of mind. Just tell yourself often enough that you can do something and you will be able to do it.'

I began to walk towards the bus stop. 'I can do it. I can do it. I can do it,' I said to myself. I began to feel the confidence flowing back into me.

I looked towards the girl. I could see her face quite clearly now. She was looking straight at me and she was smiling.

2

Linda Addison watched with interest the figure who turned the corner. He was about the same age as her, maybe a year older. He had short brown hair which was cut rather unfashionably. He was wearing a school uniform which she didn't recognise and carrying a school bag. But what was odd about him was the way that he walked. He seemed to swagger about the pavement, looking up into the air as if he were drunk.

Suddenly he stopped dead, turned abruptly at right angles and began staring into a shop window. Linda looked at her watch. The bus was due in six minutes' time.

She went back to watching the boy with the silly swagger. Now he appeared to be talking to himself. He was clearly getting quite agitated. He seemed to be shaking his fist at someone. Perhaps he was not quite right in the head.

He seemed to have come to some sort of decision. He turned towards the bus stop and began walking towards it. Linda wanted to laugh. He looked so ridiculous the way he swaggered. Perhaps there was something wrong with his legs, she thought to herself. Perhaps it was something he couldn't help, in which case she really ought not to laugh, or even smile.

She looked at her watch. Only three minutes before the bus was due. Perhaps it would be on time today. That would make a nice change.

She looked up. The boy was only a short distance from the bus stop now and he was walking towards her. He was looking directly at her and there was a strange look on his face. He stopped in front of her and opened his mouth as if to speak.

But what he said all came out in a rush, something about a cinema. Linda decided he must be asking where the cinema was.

'It's in the middle of town,' she told him, 'next to the shopping precinct. You need to get a bus on the other side of the road.'

He just stood there, looking at her in silence. Perhaps he hadn't understood.

'Any bus will do,' she told him.

'What I wanted to...' he began, but a noisy lorry went past and the sentence trailed off into something she could not hear.

'What?' she asked him.

He shook his head sadly. His shoulders began to droop.

He was making Linda feel embarrassed. Whatever was the matter with him?

It was just then that the 108b bus drew up.

'I'm sorry,' she told him. 'I have to get on this bus. It's the other side of the road if you want the cinema.'

The bus doors opened and she got on. She showed the bus driver her pass and went and sat at the back. The doors closed and the bus pulled away from the stop.

Linda turned in the seat and looked out of the window. She saw the boy standing there staring after the bus hopelessly. Then he bent down and opened his school bag. He took something out and straightened up again.

It was getting hard now to see what he was doing. There was a lot of traffic in the way, but it looked like a book that he had taken out of the bag. He seemed to be trying to rip it in half but it was too difficult for him. He struggled, pulling at it furiously with both hands. Then the bus began to turn left. She caught one last glimpse of him throwing the book onto the ground, then he was gone. She turned round on the seat and dismissed him from her mind.

Activity

Which person are these two stories written in? Which version did you prefer? How did the person used affect your view of the characters of Damian and Linda? When the first person is used, it has been said that the reader has to be more suspicious of what is said. Do you agree with this?

Investigate

Carefully study the books you have read recently. Which are written in the third person? Which in the first person? Are there any written in the second person? Which person is most often used?

six TELLING AND SELLING

Starting point

Written language changes considerably depending on who is going to read it. These holiday brochures have various features:

- they use many headings
- they use lists of points to summarise the various options available
- they use charts to make information clear
- they contain strong photographs to communicate certain messages to the reader

Royal Oak enjoys an unrivalled lake-side position at Llangorse, with stunning views of the Brecon Beacons National Park across the lake. This is home of the Royal Yachting Association approved Llangorse Sailing School, which is operated by PGL, but its proximity to a wide range of activity facilities in the area means there's so much more to Royal Oak than watersports! Accommodation at the centre is in attractive new leisure homes, each of which is divided into 2–4 berth bedrooms, with a communal lounge area. Showers and toilets are in a central block, and other amenities include a dining hall, coffee bar/large recreation room, two drying rooms and the Manager's office. The residential section of the centre is set well away from the lake-side, and is illuminated at night for ease of access between facilities. The lake acts as the focal point for PGL watersport activities in the Llangorse area. In the same way, most of the land-based activities, such as abseiling, archery and rifle shooting, take place at our Tan Troed Activity Centre, just a short drive away. The more expansive activities, like pony trekking and mountain trail, take place on the slopes of the Black Mountains, all in all a wonderful backdrop for this exciting set-programme Pacesetter holiday.

Investigate

Get hold of a range of holiday brochures for different kinds of holiday, some for adults, some for people of your own age. In what ways are the language and layout different? How are they similar?

The language of advertising

Advertisements on hoardings and on television have developed a special kind of language designed to catch the public's attention. Many of the words and expressions used have become part of the English language.

Advertisers try to convince the public that their product is better than anyone else's. This is why their language often uses **comparatives** and **superlatives**. A comparative, as its name suggests, is a word that compares something with something else, for example 'Persil washes whiter' (than other brands). Comparatives are made by adding the suffix '-er' or by using 'more'. A superlative is a word that suggests it is the best or at the top of the scale, for example 'Persil washes whitest'. Superlatives are made by adding the suffix '-est' or using 'most'.

Another feature of advertising language is the way it uses slogans, or short memorable expressions describing a product. For example, 'Heineken refreshes the parts other beers cannot reach.'

Activity

In groups, see how many of the following slogans you recognise. What products were they advertising? Do you use any of these expressions?

MAKE YOUR MAN A FLORA MAN

TOP BREEDERS RECOMMEND IT

OPAL FRUITS, MADE TO MAKE YOUR MOUTH WATER

TYPHOO, TEA YOU CAN REALLY TASTE

LET THE TRAIN TAKE THE STRAIN

THERE'S NOTHING QUITE LIKE A McDONALDS

LET YOUR FINGERS DO THE WALKING

How many other slogans can you think of which are in use now? What do you think makes a good slogan?

As well as producing memorable phrases which sometimes enter our everyday language, advertising language has other special features:

1 It uses comparatives and superlatives, for example 'Nothing acts faster than Anadin'.
2 It uses the present tense to suggest that something is happening now and is so good that it will always continue to happen, for example 'Mr Kipling bakes exceedingly good cakes'.
3 It uses the past tense to underline the fact that the product is reliable and has been successfully used for a long time, for example 'We've lapped the world with tread to spare'.
4 It uses the imperative (the form of a verb which tells you to do something), for example 'Have a break, have a KitKat'.
5 One of the most interesting features is the way in which new words are invented, for example 'cookability'.

Activity

Can you think of any new words which have been invented for advertising slogans? How many different examples of the features of advertising language listed above can you think of? Make a list of them.

According to one study, the ten most popular adjectives used in advertising are:

1 **NEW**
2 GOOD/BETTER/**BEST**
3 **FREE**
4 **Fresh**
5 **delicious**
6 **FULL**
7 **SURE**
8 CLEAN
9 ***wonderful***
10 ***SPECIAL***

Activity

Make up a series of slogans of your own:

a to sell your school to prospective pupils
b to sell your school to prospective parents
c to stop smoking
d to sell a new diet drink
e to sell a toothpaste which actually repairs cavities
f to sell an idea you believe in

Try using some of the words and techniques listed on the previous pages.

The language of newspapers

Journalists, like advertising copy-writers, are trying to get the attention of readers. One way they do this is by writing short, snappy, easy-to-read sentences. There are a large variety of newspapers in Britain and each one takes a slightly different view of how to use English.

Broadly speaking there are two kinds of newspaper, **tabloid** newspapers such as *The Daily Mirror* and **broadsheets** like *The Guardian*. A tabloid paper is smaller than the larger broadsheet size.

Read these versions of a story which appeared in a number of newspapers on 20 June 1992.

Public school expels 10

A public school has expelled ten boys after pupils went on the rampage in an end-of-exams drinking binge. Three boys were also suspended from the £9,500-a-year Hurstpierpoint College, Hassocks, West Sussex, after the incident. Headmaster Simon Watson said he had no choice but to call in police after a common room bar was broken into and drink worth £700 stolen. Boys also broke into another pupil's study on the same night and beat him up. "There can be no excuse and no justification for the behaviour that we have experienced," Mr Watson said in a letter to parents.

The Times

School expels 10 pupils for drinks theft

Ten pupils have been expelled from a private school for stealing drinks valued at £790 for an all-night party.

The sixth-formers at Hurstpierpoint College, West Sussex, broke into a staff common room to steal bottles of spirits. Some later attacked another boy in his room.

One of the 10 has been questioned by police and four others have been suspended from the school. Mr Simon Watson, the headmaster, said the boys have been allowed to return for A-level exams.

The Daily Telegraph

10 pupils expelled

TEN boys have been expelled and three suspended from a top private school after a night of theft, booze and violence.

A sixth-form gang broke into the staff bar and stole spirits worth £750.

They dumped some and other pupils then got drunk at £10,000-a-year Hurstpierpoint College, West Sussex.

Another gang attacked a pupil and cut off his hair. One boy is charged with burglary.

The Sun

The Daily Mail

End of term hangover

By PETER BURDEN

The school badge

HEAD CALLS IN POLICE AFTER SIXTH-FORMERS STEAL DRINK

A PUBLIC school head refused to regard it as an end-of-term prank when pupils stole drink from the masters' common room.

He reported it to the police as a burglary.

Senior pupils were questioned by officers at Hurstpierpoint College, Hassocks, West Sussex. Another boy, who had already left for the summer holidays, was arrested and bailed.

He and five other sixth-formers were then expelled. Two more were suspended.

Head Simon Watson said yesterday: 'It's been jolly uncomfortable for me but we stand for standards.'

Most of the pupils at the £10,000-a-year school — motto: Blessed are the Pure in Heart — are boarders. Mr Watson said the common room had been broken into in a 'spur of the moment challenge by pupils who had reached the end of their school careers'.

He added: 'It was no end-of-term prank. Considerable force was used and some £700 of stock stolen from the bar. Only part has been recovered since much was consumed by senior boys.'

In another incident the same night, which Mr Watson said was unrelated, a group of boys broke into a pupil's study and 'set upon' him. Mr Watson said they wanted to 'teach him a lesson' after he cut the hair of a sleeping fifth-former. For that, four sixth-formers were expelled and two boys suspended.

All but one of the expelled boys were within a few days of leaving the College. Special arrangements have been made for them to sit their A-levels.

Activity

Which headline do you think is most effective and why? What differences can you find between the language used to describe the way the boys behaved, the kind of school it was and the seriousness of the incident?

Investigate

Collect as many newspapers as you can from one particular day. Choose a story which you find interesting and follow it through in the different papers.

Study the ways in which:

a people are described and introduced (Are you told their class, race, age, gender, looks, and so on?).

b women are treated (Are they described in the same way as men?).

c other countries are described (Are they all treated in the same way?).

d words are used (How long are they? Are there any favourite words? Is slang ever used?).

e headlines are written (Are they simple or clever?).

The language of special interests

Large areas of countryside are destroyed to build road systems like this one.

Photochemical smog, Transvaal, South Africa.

Expressions like 'photochemical smog' are increasingly being used in connection with the environment. In fact there is a whole new vocabulary of words which try to describe our concerns for the environment.

Investigate

Look at the titles of books about the environment in your school library. Look in the fiction section, as well as on the non-fiction shelves. Make up your own list of 'eco-words'. Do you think it is necessary to have special words like this?

The environment is not the only area of special interest which has developed its own language. There are many other areas of your life where specialist vocabularies are used.

City streets clogged with traffic, Bangkok, Thailand.

Acid rain damage in China.

Air pollution – the decomposed stonework of Canterbury Cathedral.

Judge.

Scientist.

Weatherman.

Doctor.

Investigate

Find examples of writing in these specialist areas: weather-forecasting, medicine, science, law and computing. Make up lists of key words which are special to them. Produce your own definitions for these words.

The language of rules and instructions

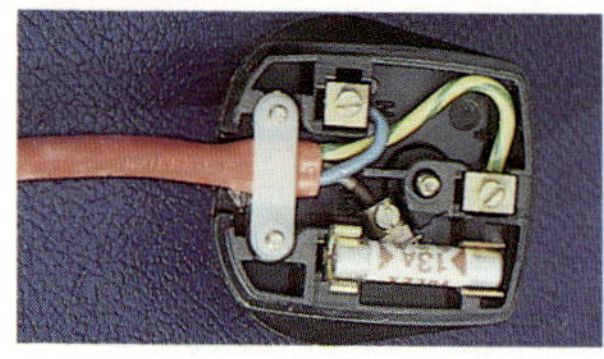

It is difficult to cope without being able to read and understand instructions. Whether it is understanding directions to get to a friend's house or learning a new game, we need them.

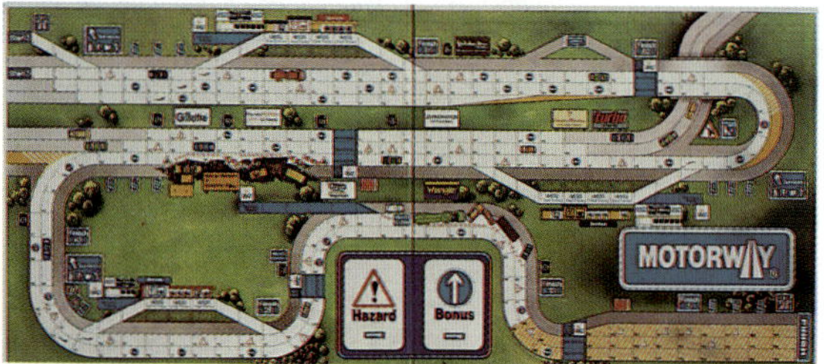

Good, clear instructions tend to be numbered or clearly organised into groups of sentences. They are normally simple sentences, like 'No letter may be moved after it has been played', or imperatives like 'Keep a tally of each player's score'.

Look at this example taken from a well-known game, *Scrabble*.

SCRABBLE®

THE WORLD'S LEADING WORD GAME

RULES OF PLAY

Scrabble is a word game for 2, 3 or 4 players. Play consists of forming interlocking words, cross-word fashion, on the Scrabble playing board, using letter tiles with various score values. Each player competes for the highest score by using his tiles in combinations and locations that take best advantage of letter values and premium squares on the board. The combined total score for a game may range from about 400 points to 800 or more depending on the skill of the players.

To Begin

Turn all tiles face down at the side of the board, or put them into the bag provided, and shuffle. Draw for first play. The player drawing the tile nearest the beginning of the alphabet plays first. Put the exposed tiles back and reshuffle. Each player then draws seven new tiles and places them on his rack.

One player is elected as scorekeeper. He may also take part in the game.

Method of Play

1. The first player combines two or more of his tiles to form a word and places them on the board to read either across or down with one tile on the centre square (star).

2. A player completes his turn by counting and announcing his score for the turn which is recorded by the scorekeeper (see 11). He then draws as many new tiles as he has played, thus always keeping seven tiles in his rack.

3. Play then passes to the left. The second player, then each in turn, adds one or more tiles to those already played so as to form new words.

All tiles played in any one turn must be placed in one row across or down the board. Diagonal words are not permitted. The tiles played must form one complete word and if, at the same time, they touch other tiles in adjacent rows, they must form complete words cross-word fashion, with all such tiles. The player gets full credit for all words formed or modified by his play.

4. **New words** may be formed by:

a) Adding one or more tiles to a word already on the board.

b) Placing a word at right angles to a word already on the board. The new word must use one of the letters of the word already on the board or must add a letter to it (turns 2 and 4, page 5). It may also "bridge" two or more words (see example page 6).

c) Placing a complete word parallel to a word already

2

played so that adjoining tiles also form complete words (see Guide Game, turn 11).

5. No tile may be shifted after it has been played.

6. The two **blank tiles** may be used as any letter desired. When playing a blank the player must state what letter it represents, after which it cannot be changed during the game.

7. Any player may use his turn to **replace** any or all of the **tiles** in his rack. He does so by discarding them face down, drawing the same number of new tiles, then mixing the discarded tiles with those remaining in the pool. He then awaits his next turn to play.

Instead of placing tiles on the board, or exchanging tiles, a player may also **pass**, whether or not he is able to make a word (or words).

However, should all players pass twice in succession, the game ends.

8. **Permitted Words:** Any words listed in a standard English dictionary are permitted except those only spelt with an initial capital letter, abbreviations, prefixes and suffixes and words requiring apostrophes and hyphens. Foreign words in a standard English dictionary are considered to have been absorbed into the English language and are allowed. Consult a dictionary only to check spelling or usage. Any word may be challenged before the next player starts his turn. If the word challenged is unacceptable, the player takes back his tiles and loses his turn.

9. The **game ends** when all the tiles have been drawn and one of the players has used all the tiles in his rack. The game also ends when all possible plays have been made or all players have passed twice in consecutive turns.

Scoring

10. The scorekeeper keeps a tally of each player's score, entering it after each turn on the scorepad. The **score value** of each letter is indicated by a number at the bottom of the tile. The score value of a blank is zero.

3

11. The score for each turn is the sum of the score values of all the tiles in each word formed or modified in that turn plus the premium values resulting from placing tiles on premium squares.

12. **Premium Letter Squares:** A light blue square doubles the score of a letter placed on it; a dark blue square trebles the letter score.

13. **Premium Word Squares:** The score for the entire word is doubled when one of its tiles is placed on a light red square; it is trebled when a tile is placed on a dark red square. Include premiums for double or triple letter values, if any, before doubling or trebling the word score.

If a word is formed that covers two premium word squares, the score is doubled then re-doubled (4 times letter score), or trebled and then re-trebled (9 times letter score) as the case may be.

Note that the centre square (star) is a light red square and therefore doubles the score for the first word.

14. The above letter and word premiums apply only in the turn in which they are first played. In subsequent turns tiles count at face value.

15. When a blank tile falls on a light red or a dark red square, the sum of the tiles in the word is doubled or trebled even though the blank itself has no score value.

16. When two or more words are formed in the same turn, each is scored. The common letter is counted (with full premium value, if any) in the score for each word. (See examples, turns 3 and 4 on page 5).

17. Any player who plays all seven of his tiles in a single turn scores a premium of 50 points in addition to his regular score for the turn. The 50 points are added on **after** doubling or tripling a word score. (See Guide Game, turn 19).

18. At the end of the game each player's score is reduced by the sum of his unplayed tiles, and if one player has used all his tiles, his score is increased by the sum of the unplayed tiles of all the other players.

4

Activity

In pairs, choose an activity that you both know well, such as cleaning your teeth, which can be undertaken in the classroom. Then take it in turns to give the other person clear instructions while he or she does what you say.

There is a group called Plain English which campaigns to keep English short, simple and easy to understand. They have found many examples of instructions which are very difficult to follow. Each year Golden Bull awards are made to the worst offenders, like a letter from an insurance officer which began:

> As insurance officer I have decided to review the decision dated 19.9.83 for the following reasons: that by its decision of 31.1.84 the medical board varied the assessment of disablement resulting from the relevant loss of faculty and this constitutes a revision of a decision on a special question.

Investigate

Find a set of rules which, in your opinion, is difficult to follow and re-word it so that it is made up of clear instructions.

The language of school

The time you have spent at school so far will have made you an expert in the language used at school, especially that used by teachers!

Read this extract from a play by John Godber called *Teechers*.

GAIL Are we doing this play or what?

SALTY It's like when she gets you in her office, all neat and smelling of perfume, and she says, 'You don't come to school to fool around, Ian, to waste your time. We treat you like young adults and we expect you to behave accordingly. I don't think that writing on a wall is a mature thing to do.'

HOBBY That's good that, Salty, just like her.

SALTY Yeh, but really she wants to say, 'Hey, Salty, pack all this graffiti in, it's getting on my knackers.'

GAIL Are we starting?

SALTY Anyway, why am I bothered? No more school, no more stick, no more teachers thinking that you're thick...

GAIL No more of Miss Jubb shouting like you're deaf as a post, 'Gail Saunders, how dare you belch in front of me.' Sorry, miss, didn't know it was your turn ...

HOBBY Brilliant...

GAIL Oh, and no more scenes in changing rooms where you daren't get changed because you wear a vest and everyone has got a bra...

HOBBY No more Mr Thorn sending letters home about how I missed games and was seen eating a kebab in the Golden Spoon.

GAIL No more sweaty geog teachers with Brylcreem Hush Puppies.

SALTY No more trendy art teachers, who say, 'Hiya' and, 'Call me Gordon'...

HOBBY We haven't had an art teacher called Gordon.

SALTY I know.

Activity

Do you recognise any of these expressions? In groups, make a list of things which teachers typically say:

a at the start of lessons
b at the end of lessons
c when they are angry

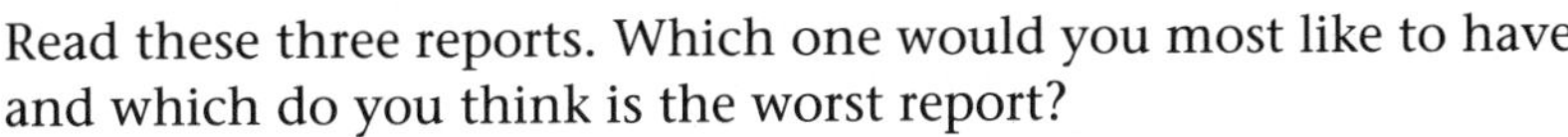

Read these three reports. Which one would you most like to have and which do you think is the worst report?

ATTITUDE TO LEARNING

Janice can work well in certain areas of the curriculum, but she is sometimes distracted and occasionally finds it difficult to concentrate on a task. She needs to be encouraged to use all of her ability and to contribute more when working in a group. When her interest is engaged, she will seek approval from the teacher and then respond well to encouragement and praise. However, in general, she is capable of greater all round commitment – this would ensure that her full potential is realised.

ENGLISH

Lee is able to respond to stories, but he does not always listen to instructions. He is able to express his point of view clearly, can articulate his feelings and he has a developing vocabulary. But at times he finds it difficult to differentiate between real or imaginary events, or to place them in a connected narrative. He needs to concentrate more on what is being said and to develop his interactive skills.

ENGLISH

Susan has a developing vocabulary in different areas of the curriculum. She is able to express her point of view clearly and articulates her feelings. She is able to listen attentively to instructions and responds to stories, poems, rhymes and songs. She can talk clearly about experiences in or out of school, and can relate real or imaginary events. She likes to make up stories and act them out, and often initiates this kind of activity. She can recite poems or songs which she has learned by heart, and can retell a familiar story. She can ask and answer questions, convey a simple message and is able to understand and give simple explanations. She is able to plan activities with other members of a group and listen to their contributions.

Activity

Which words occur in more than one report? Are they 'school' words, or do you use them elsewhere? Look up any words you do not understand. Write your own English report, using some of the words and ideas above.

Do you think these reports are clear? Which words or sentences do you find difficult to understand? Look closely at the line in Janice's report: 'She needs to be encouraged to use all of her ability'. What do you think it might mean?

Rewrite one of the reports above so that no one of your age will be in any doubt about what it means.

The language of ceremony

A Japanese wedding ceremony.

One of the ceremonies which many people experience is the marriage service.

Read these extracts from the traditional Christian wedding service in the *Book of Common Prayer*.

Then shall the Curate say unto the Man,
Wilt thou have this woman to thy wedded wife, to live together with God's ordinance in the holy estate of Matrimony? Wilt thou love her, comfort her, honour, and keep her, in sickness and in health; and, forsaking all other, keep thee only unto her, so long as ye both shall live?

The Man shall answer,
I will.

Then shall the Priest say unto the Woman,
Wilt thou have this man to thy wedded husband, to live together after God's ordinance in the holy estate of Matrimony? Wilt thou obey him, and serve him, love, honour, and keep him, in sickness and in health; and, forsaking all other, keep thee only unto him, so long as ye both shall live?

The Woman shall answer,
I will.

And the Priest, taking the Ring, shall deliver it unto the Man, to put it upon the fourth finger of the Woman's left hand. And the Man holding the Ring there, and taught by the Priest, shall say,
With this ring I thee wed, with my body I thee worship, and with all my worldly goods I thee endow: In the Name of the Father, and of the Son, and of the Holy Ghost.

This service is still used by some people today, yet few people would go around saying 'thee' or 'ye'. Words which are no longer used in normal communication are called **archaisms**.

A wedding in Fiji.

Activity

What do you notice about the language of this ceremony? How many archaisms can you find? Why do you think people like to use words which are out of date? Do you think the sound of the words is important? Do you agree with what the words say? Would you want to have this marriage ceremony yourself?

The ceremony of the Dunmow Flitch is an ancient custom celebrated in Dunmow in Essex. A flitch of bacon is presented to married couples who can prove that, for a year and a day, they have not regretted their marriage. The judge asks them to swear that this is true, using the following words:

You shall swear by custom of confession
If ever you made nuptial transgression
Be you either married man or wife
If you have brawls or contentious strife;
Or otherwise at bed or board
Offended each other in deed or word:
You wished yourself unmarried again;
Or in a twelvemonth and a day
Repented not in thought in any way;
But continued true in thought and desire
As when you joined hands in the quire;
If to these conditions without all fear
Of your own accord you will freely swear
A whole gammon of bacon you shall receive
And bear it hence with love and good leave:
For this is our custom at Dunmow well-known
Though the pleasure be ours, the bacon's your own.

Activity

What are the main features of the language used in this ceremony? Make up a ceremony of your own to celebrate a year and a day of something which is important to you, such as a year and a day of being at a new school.

Investigate

How many different types of marriage ceremony can you find from different cultures and religions? How do they differ? In what ways are they similar?

A Greek Orthodox wedding.

Resources

Useful books

General

Cambridge Encyclopaedia of English, ed. David Crystal, Cambridge University Press
Lingo, Spooner, Duckworths
Our Greek and Latin Roots, James Morwood and Mark Warman, Cambridge University Press
The Languages Book, English and Media Centre
The Story of English, Robert McCrum, William Cran and Robert MacNeil, Faber & Faber/BBC

Origins of words

Dictionary of English Place Names, ed. A D Mills, Oxford University Press
Dictionary of Eponyms, ed. Beeching, Oxford University Press
Encyclopaedia of Word and Phrase Origins, ed. Hendrickson, Macmillan
Thesaurus of English Words and Phrases, ed. Roget, Longman
Oxford Dictionary of New Words, ed. Sarah Tulloch, Oxford University Press
The Word Book, Gyles Brandreth, Robson Books

Rhymes and riddles

Children's Games in Street and Playground, I. and P. Opie, Oxford University Press
Come Hither, Walter de la Mare, Constable & Co.
Oxford Dictionary of Nursery Rhymes, ed. I. and P. Opie, Oxford University Press

Reference

Oxford English Dictionary, ed. Simpson and Weiner, Oxford University Press
Thesaurus, ed. Roget, Longman

Useful addresses

Esperanto Centre, 140 Holland Park Avenue, London W11 4UF
National Viewers and Listeners Association, Blackernae, Ardleigh, Colchester, Essex CO7 7RH

Index of knowledge about language terms

Acknowledgements

Thanks are due to the following for permission to reproduce from copyright material:

page **6**: extract from the *Oxford Junior Dictionary*, Oxford University Press; page **11**: extract from *The Knight's Tale* by Geoffrey Chaucer, Cambridge University Press; page 20: 'Comma lost nurse job' reproduced from *English in the Making 1* by Tom Peryer, Cambridge University Press; page **21**: selection of proof correction symbols reproduced with permission from BSI Standards (*BS 5261 Part 2*, 1976); page **31**: 'Poem' by Mike Rosen; pages **36–7**: extract from *Can you Sue your Parents for Malpractice?* by Paula Danziger, Dell Publishing; page **41**: extract from Winston Churchill's speech, Hansard *Fifth series, issue no. 1096, volume 360, 13 May, 1940, cl. 1501 to col. 1502*, HMSO; page **42**: extract from the speech by Martin Luther King, Jr. 'I have a dream', reprinted from *What Manner of Man: a Biography of Martin Luther King* by Lerone Bennett, George Allen & Unwin, now Unwin Hyman, an imprint of HarperCollins Publishers Limited; page **44**: extract from *Is that it?* by Bob Geldof, reproduced with permission of the author; page **51**: 'So say the lads an' lasses' reprinted from the *Education Guardian*, © *The Guardian*; page **52**: 'Prince of Wales says English is taught bloody badly' reprinted from *The Times*, Thursday 29 June 1989; page **77**: 'The Renaming story' reprinted from *English in the Making 1* by Tom Peryer, Cambridge University Press; page **79**: *A Glance at Esperanto* and page **81**: *La famili-o* reproduced by permission of the Esperanto Centre, London; page **90**: extract from *Punjabi Nursery Rhymes* by Manju Bhatia, Mantra Publishing Ltd; pages **94–5**: extract from *Hieroglyphs and Alphabets* by Charles King, published by Random House UK Limited; page **96**: *Scrabble* reproduced with kind permission of J W Spear & Sons Plc, Enfield, Middlesex; page **99**: *The Star* by H G Wells; pages **100–1**: extract from *New Guys Around the Block* by Rosa Guy, published by Victor Gollancz; page **102**: extract from *Isaac Campion* © 1986 Janni Howker, permission granted by the publishers, Walker Books Limited; page **105**: extract from *Carrie's War* by Nina Bawden, published by Victor Gollancz; page **106**: extracts from *The Catalogue of the Universe* by Margaret Mahy, J M Dent & Sons Ltd, Publishers; page **112**: Butlins Holidays; page **113**: PGL Adventure Holidays; page **114**: British Railways Board; McDonald's; Premier Brands; Bourneville; copyright British Telecommunications plc in the UK; Van den Bergh Foods Limited; Mars UK Limited; page **116**: articles reprinted from *The Times*, and *The Sun*, 10 June 1992; page **117**: 'End of term hangover' reprinted from *The Daily Mail*; page **120**: *Scrabble* reproduced by kind permission of J W Spear & Sons Plc, Enfield, Middlesex; page **124**: extract from *Teechers* by John Godber.

Every effort has been made to reach copyright holders. The publishers would be glad to hear from anyone whose rights they have unknowingly infringed.